VICKI FOOTE

MOOR TO SEA

A Journey Along
The Cleveland Way

Printed in Australia

Cover by Agata Buiko

Map design by Ross Healey

Edited by Samantha Elley

Internal design by Coven Press www.covenpress.com.au

Images in this book are copyright approved for use by author

First printing: July 2025

Paperback ISBN 978-0-6467-1315-1

eBook ISBN 978-0-6467-1726-5

www.footenotes.net.au

 A catalogue record for this work is available from the National Library of Australia

Distributed by Lightning Source Global

'It's your road, and yours alone.
Others may walk it with you,
but no-one can walk it for you.'

Rumi

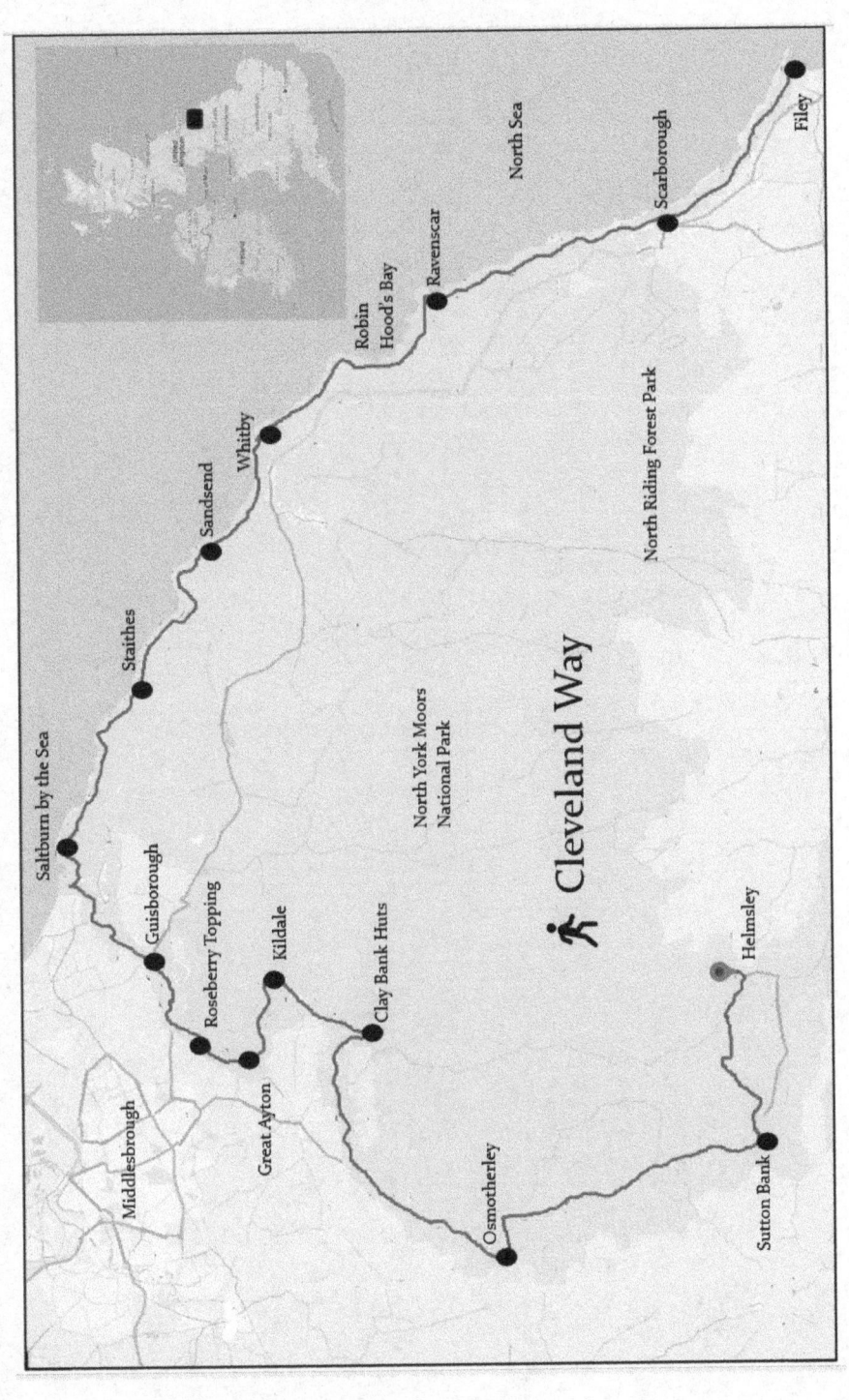

ARRIVE HELMSLEY

"Fancy a cider?" Olaf asked.

"Hell, yes! Absolutely. We deserve it," I replied.

"Two ciders it is. Back in a tick."

We'd made it. We'd arrived in Helmsley with a 175-kilometre walk ahead of us and a life-changing journey behind us. It was incredible to be at the 'starting line' of the Cleveland Way in Yorkshire, ready to tackle it over the next nine days – assuming all went to plan, of course. That plan was clearly to finish the walk but it went way beyond that. It had been the most powerful gift imaginable to get me through eight months of breast cancer treatment. That plan had sustained me through the difficult days, given a tangible focus and helped me recover and heal. It had been my emotional saviour and I desperately wanted to see it through. Now, a long way from Adelaide, it wasn't just a plan anymore, it was all very real.

My parched mouth hankered for the drink as I sat outside the sun-drenched Feathers Hotel and could hardly wait for Olaf to return with it. I was a bubbling mix of excitement and anxiety at the thought of traipsing across the North York Moors, then along the North Sea coastline. It would be a challenge at the best of times but, with my final dose of chemotherapy only six weeks ago, I didn't know if my body would hold up. One medico thought it 'unlikely' I'd make it; others wryly wished me luck and an oncology nurse had said, "Most people celebrate the end of chemo with a massage or relaxing holiday, not by walking 175kms."

But his cheeky grin and wink told me he had faith in me. Right now, I wished I shared his belief.

I'd come a long way since the morning my life catapulted into a different universe but, as I waited for my thirst-quencher, a knot rose in my stomach and I was transported back to the moment I'd found the lump in my right breast. I'd woken minutes before my alarm and had snuggled into Olaf's warm and secure back when an uncomfortable jab at the front of my ribcage, where my bra underwire normally sat, immediately grabbed my attention. I hesitated before allowing myself to examine the sore spot and then, in a split-second, contented sleep became a dizzying whirlpool of disbelief, overwhelming panic and an inability to think. It was definitely a lump and it was sizeable, yet I hadn't noticed it before. *Had this lump appeared overnight? How could it have gone unnoticed when it was close to two centimetres wide?*

I was sure the loud voices in my head would wake Olaf as they duelled between insisting on staying calm and screaming out for help. But with no way of staying calm, I kept feeling the lump, praying for a different result. But it was still there; it was still sore and it was terrifying. If the loud voices didn't wake him, I was sure my thudding heart would.

"Olaf, feel this," I demanded, my fingers stabbing his shoulder. "Have you noticed it before? It's really sore."

He opened his eyes, trying to make sense of it all.

"It feels like a lump and I haven't noticed it before," he said, putting his fingers where directed, "but that doesn't mean anything." He must've felt me tense. "It's in a funny spot, so could've been there a while and neither of us noticed."

"Okay. Maybe my bra was a bit tight. God, I hope that's all it is."

"Is the other one sore?"

"No. Just this one. Oh, this can't be happening."

"It's probably nothing. Just get it checked ASAP. I'm sure there's no need to worry."

"I hope you're right." I got up, started my weekday routine and counted the minutes till I could ring my GP.

With the poking and prodding of the examination over, I stood to redress as my breath caught in my throat; a half-sigh, half-choking noise emerged. I took several deep breaths to regroup, then returned to the GP's adjoining room. She wasn't my usual doctor, in fact, I'd not seen her at the clinic before but, at such short notice, I was desperate for any appointment. The whooshing and whirring noise in my head was halted before I'd even sat down.

"I don't think it's cancer," she said confidently.

"Oh, thank God," I choked as tears flowed.

"I've seen and felt a lot of cancers over the years and yours doesn't fit the mould. It's sore and I could feel all the way around it, so I'm pretty sure it's not cancer."

"Oh! That's amazing news."

"But I want you to have a mammogram Vicki, just to make sure."

It was an enormous relief and the best news anyone could get. I'd have the mammogram just to be sure, but my mind was completely at ease. I could hear Olaf's words already, "I told you there was nothing to worry about."

But there was something to worry about. There was a LOT to worry about and my false sense of security was shattered 10 days later when the mammogram wasn't progressing as it should. There was the usual squishing and squashing but then there was the wait in a white, soulless room for an inordinate amount of time before an expressionless official-looking woman entered.

"Sorry to keep you waiting," she said, "but we need to scan your right breast again to get a clearer picture of a couple of things."

"Oh!" I managed. "That doesn't sound good."

"We just need a different angle sometimes, it's very common. There's no need to worry."

There was that phrase again. No need to worry. But after another scan, more waiting time and the need for three biopsies, worry was all I could do. Despite everyone's advice not to worry, the possibility this *could* be cancer started to become a reality.

"When do I get the results?" I asked once the procedures were over.

"Ring your GP in about 24 hours," she replied, "they'll have the results by then."

A busy day at work followed, helping to reduce my anxiety and walking the dog in the evening sunshine was a pleasurable diversion to keep my mind occupied. But despite my best efforts to 'try not to worry', it would be the longest 24 hours of my life.

I returned to the present as Olaf handed over the pint of Thatchers and plucked a packet of crisps from under his arm. He exhaled with relief and folded his 191-centimetre-tall frame into the seat beside me. It was a sigh that said, what an effort, what a time we've had, what a relief to be in Helmsley. His face was radiant in the sunlight and he looked more relaxed and maybe even younger, than he had in months.

"What are all these people doing here?" I asked.

"Turns out there's heaps of walks that either start here or pass through and apparently, it's peak season. Oh and there's quite a few recreational shooters here for a spot of hunting."

"Oh, bloody hell. I hope they don't mistake us for a pheasant or grouse on our walk tomorrow. That's a bit of a worry."

"Nah, we'll be okay. Want a crisp?" He offered the opened packet.

The cold drink was perfect and I unfurled our map of the Cleveland Way to see what lay ahead. We knew we'd need to walk about 20 kilometres a day and we knew the terrain went from moors to sea, but now we were here I wanted to prepare as best I could to give us a chance of arriving in Filey, our end point, in nine days.

But we hadn't always planned on walking the Cleveland Way, in fact, we'd never even heard of it until serendipity stepped in. By pure chance one afternoon, while searching for our perfect long-distance walk, with online sites not delivering and our dog-eared travel guides well past their prime, I was inexplicably drawn to a void on our bookshelf. Taking a closer look, I found a small orange book firmly wedged between two bigger ones, playing hide and seek. It was *The Joy of Walking* by David Bathurst, a gift I'd given Olaf years before and completely forgotten about. I flicked it open and there on page 121 were seven UK walking trails, including the Cleveland Way. And then, everything fell into place – this walk was the right distance, the right number of days, offered two walks in one and I knew it was the one for us. In no way are we serious walkers, but we *are* serious lovers of walking holidays, so we decided on the Cleveland Way and gave ourselves 10 months to prepare; nothing was going to get in our way.

"What's up?" Olaf asked. "You're not *really* worried about being mistaken for a pheasant or a partridge, are you?

"No. I'm starting to wonder if this was a really bad idea. What happens if I can't actually finish?" I replied, not sharing his humour.

"Look, there's no need to worry. If it gets too much, I'll get a frigging wheelbarrow and push you the rest of the way. Okay?"

"Oh, right! And what if your bung knee gives out? We'll need two wheelbarrows and then who's going to push?"

"Well, then we'll be buggered, I guess." His smile calmed my nerves and we chuckled. "But honestly, we're going to be fine. We'll take one day at a time and we'll be fine. Now, let's look at the route so we're ready for day one – Helmsley to Sutton Bank." He moved the map towards him and began to study it.

But I still had my doubts. I dreaded that I might stumble and not see this much-anticipated plan through. Then I reflected on sage words we'd heard from a 70-something, grieving, Irish widow named Mary, a devoted pilgrim we'd met on the Camino de Santiago de Compostela three years earlier, who'd said, "No-one else can walk your Camino."

It was powerful then and poignant now; I would have to realise this was *my* Cleveland Way and, if it meant being pushed in a wheelbarrow, that's how it would be.

Two pints down and I was now weary. There was residual jetlag from the long-haul flight from Australia, a two-hour train trip from London to York, then a 90-minute ride on the 31X bus to Helmsley to add to the mountain of anxious, uncertain energy. It had all caught up with me and I clearly needed something more substantial than crisps to provide an energy boost for the following day. Across the ancient market square, in an inviting trattoria, we loaded up on carbs in near world record time - I was ravenous and devoured a delicious risotto and Olaf's enormous bowl of pasta disappeared in a blink – we ate as though we were on some sort of time limit, but the only 'limitation' was my increasing desire for sleep, as my body clock was still adjusting to having had its time zones upended. But before that could happen, I wanted to fully prep for the morning.

I rolled up my bamboo socks and shoved them into my walking shoes, leant my walking pole against the wall and carefully lined them up facing the door. It was funny how expectant they looked and a relief that they appeared more than ready, even eager, to tackle what lay ahead. The weather was supposed to be fine, so a short-sleeved shirt and light walking pants were selected and placed near the shoes. The slightly obsessive pile I was creating almost bordering on the absurd. But I needed to feel 'in control' of at least this part of the walk and, if that meant creating a 'visualisation' scene, then that's what I needed to do.

Next – the day pack. I knew how important it was to get this right, not just what to put in it, but where it went and how accessible it was. I filled our water bottles and placed them in Olaf's pack; he was always the 'water carrier' on our walks and this time it seemed more important than ever. He didn't mind the weight and knew how vital it was for me to carry less and hopefully achieve our goal. Sunscreen, Band-Aids, lip balm, insect repellent, guidebook, map, notebook, pen, phone, cash, long-sleeved top – what had I forgotten? Oh, yes – a hat. I'd really be needing that with my thin, blonde, wispy hair not providing much coverage yet. All the essentials were strategically packed, except the cheese knife.

"The cheese!" I yelled.

"Don't panic. It's already in the kitchen fridge," Olaf said. "We can grab it whenever we want."

"Oh, thank goodness we remembered. And when I say *we*, I mean *you*."

"Well, I'm the one carrying it, I assume, so I'm happy to keep it as fresh as possible."

"Okay then, you get to choose our cheese for tomorrow. Snack-bearer's choice – only seems fair."

"Do I have to do that now or can I sleep on it?"

"Sleep on it but I hope it doesn't give you weird dreams."

"Me too. We both need a really good sleep tonight. Now, sweet ones." He rolled over and my heart swelled with this nightly sign-off.

En route to Helmsley, we'd had a one-day stop in London with a mission to use a £50 gift voucher at Neal's Yard Dairy – a thoughtful, recent birthday present from a close friend.

We lucked on London's most passionate cheesemonger in the Covent Garden shop who loved our Cleveland Way plans and revelled in tailoring the bounty for longevity and portability. I watched in awe at his masterful wrapping skills as he deftly swaddled wedges of semi-hard Montgomery's Cheddar, full-bodied Appleby's Cheshire, Gouda-like Coolea and the soft goat's milk Innes Log in long-lasting wax paper. That haul would perfectly pair with English Quince & Damson Paste, Colvin's Pepper Jelly and a selection of crackers, he advised.

"Will it survive in our backpacks crossing the moors?" I asked. "Will it last for nine days?"

"It'll last pretty well if you treat it right," he said. "Don't forget, farmers used to lug chunks of cheddar for days in their saddlebags. They'd stop for lunch and voilà! Delicious. So, your cheeses will be fine. And you can put *yours* in a fridge at night."

"Well, one thing's for sure, we won't go hungry," Olaf said.

"Not even if you get yourselves lost. Go well," he said as we left.

There's no way we'd be getting lost. I brushed off the comment and practically skipped along the footpath elated at the armoury any cheese-lover would delight in. I loved cheese so much, I had to have been a mouse in a previous life. But in more recent times, the thing mice and I had in common was not just a love of cheese, it was also the fear of being trapped – for them in a mousetrap, for me by illness – and that was something I was determined to avoid.

LONGEST 24 HOURS

An early start to work was a total blessing. I didn't even mind the usual daily grind of monitoring the radio for political stories. Today, it was a much-needed distraction. The hours whizzed by through a procession of transcripts and, before I knew it, the clock had ticked over to afternoon. When I registered what the voice at the back of my mind meant, dread gripped my stomach as I debated when would be the best time to call for my results. Eventually, the need to know overtook and I dialled the number.

My heart rate skyrocketed with my GP's greeting, the thumping in my chest matched only by the pounding in my head. I could barely find enough voice to speak. Then, to make matters worse, my scan results hadn't arrived and my long-time doctor vowed to follow up immediately. For a nanosecond, I was filled with relief, subscribing to the 'no news is good news' philosophy, but that was soon engulfed by a desperate desire to know. I tried to sound breezy as I signed off, but it couldn't have been further from the truth. It was going to be a difficult wait and even harder to focus on work.

For 20 minutes, which went both glacially slow and simultaneously at warp speed, my mind wavered between absolute confidence that everything was fine and the unfathomable prospect of a bad diagnosis. I sat at my desk in a cocoon, enveloped in contemplative isolation, totally detached from reality and completely oblivious to any media stories I should've been across for the new premier and his fledgling ministers. Anything could've happened around me and I wouldn't have known or cared. I was numb and unaware of life beyond this bubble of confusion and, although I'd already been waiting 24 hours, this extra time took an eternity.

When the call finally came, I hesitated to answer – this was the moment it was all going to be okay or it was the moment my life would change forever – and I scurried around the open-plan space, past dozens of desk-bound workers, looking for somewhere private. The ringtone seemed to become more urgent as the unanswered seconds ticked by, so when I reached the floor's empty lift foyer, I slid the green phone icon to the right and offered a carefree greeting. But within seconds, that bravado was replaced by a wave of nausea and fear on hearing my GP's tone.

Without hesitation, he softly said, "I'm sorry Vicki, but you have malignancies in your right breast."

I was silent. I couldn't respond. I couldn't think. I couldn't even breathe. He probably continued speaking but all I could hear was whooshing in my ears. A woman emerged from the nearest lift, smiled at me then mouthed 'hello' but I stared straight through her and turned away. A chatting duo, holding containers of food, walked past heading for the kitchen and the inappropriateness of my surrounds was obvious. Was a lift foyer the ideal place to be told I had cancer? It's not what I would've ever imagined but, then again, I never imagined it would happen to me.

Amid the foot traffic of comings and goings to meetings, others to the bathroom and some heading down for a smoko, the shock and chaos in my brain temporarily paused and I homed in on just one word – malignancies. He'd either intentionally or accidentally *not* used the 'c' word, but if it was meant to soften the blow, all it did was confuse me and I wondered if I even had cancer. Perhaps that harsh-sounding word meant something different to the medical profession. Maybe I'd assumed it meant cancer when it didn't. Or was it the other word that was the bad one? Which one was it - malignant or benign? Think, think, think. But thinking was beyond me and when my scattered attention managed to re-focus, it was just as the doctor said something about lymph nodes being clear which, he said, was excellent news.

I wanted to rewind the conversation and start over again, to listen forensically to each syllable and find where he said I would be okay. But as the lift lobby cleared and fell silent, the voice at the other end continued and all I heard was, "I'm sorry," and "terrible news." That's when it hit me – I had breast cancer. I was *that* person. It was real. It was me. SHIT!

I stumbled on an unused meeting room and sat staring into space and made the next call.

"So, how'd you go? All clear?" Olaf asked.

"No. *Not* all clear. It's not good. In fact, it doesn't get any worse. And I can't think straight and don't know what to do," I replied, my throat sore from the lump that was forming there as I spoke.

"Oh shit. Right. Okay. Where are you? You're not still at work, are you?"

"Yes, I'm still here but I've got to get out of this place. I'm feeling hemmed in and need fresh air. I'm going to grab my gear and go."

"Head into Victoria Square and I can be there in half an hour."

"No. I can't wait that long. I need to keep moving. I'll just catch the bus and see you at home."

"Are you sure you're-," But I'd already hung up. I had to get out of there. I needed to breathe. I'd see him at home.

Olaf stood, ashen-faced, on the veranda, waiting and I ran to him, dropping an armful of bags and flung myself into his arms which he locked around my back. We didn't speak, just breathed deeply together and I prayed for time to stand still. Being in his arms was the safest place in the world, of security and comfort and, if we could freeze that moment forever, everything would be fine. And then my tears came with loud, giant sobs into his chest, my body spasming between each gasp, as he stroked my hair and held me tight.

Together we were strong and would tackle whatever lay ahead. First up, it was a hastily made appointment with the breast surgeon who, I hoped, would have some positive news. Perhaps it wasn't all doom and gloom. Had I catastrophised the earlier phone call and it would actually be okay? Facing an even longer 24 hours than I'd just been through, my fate would be revealed tomorrow.

Day 1
HELMSLEY TO SUTTON BANK
16 kilometres

I woke, abuzz with excitement and trepidation, as a gap in the curtains allowed in streaks of morning light. It was 5:15am and I was delighted to have had a few solid hours' sleep. It was too early to get up and charge into the day although, clearly, the birds outside didn't agree, so I closed my eyes again hoping to entice a bit more rest. But that meant trying to put aside the second guessing I felt about my preparedness for this quest. It was one thing to have willed my way here, but healing was operating at its own pace and my stamina was a big unknown. If my physicality faltered because I hadn't trained enough or my recovering muscles were more vulnerable to injury and strain, I had no second string to my bow and the idea of potentially hoisting a white flag in surrender kept rearing its persistent head.

Olaf was in the depths of sleep beneath the floral-patterned quilt and clearly didn't share my level of anxiety. Thank goodness one of us was confident the next nine days would be okay – challenging yes, but he'd assured me it would be fine.

After another hour of restless ruminating, I got up and started preparing for our adventure. The sound of my shower must've woken Olaf because when I returned from the bathroom, he was rummaging in his bag.

"I think I'll wear this today," he said, holding up his new blue shirt, "for luck."

"Oh, right. Do you think we'll need luck?" I asked.

"No, probably not. But it can't hurt. If it helps us get through day one, I'll be happy."

"Yeah, me too. I know it's only 16ks but I'd like it to go smoothly to kind of ease us into it."

"It'll be fine. We'll be fine."

We made some last-minute adjustments to our kit and then Olaf had to make the big decision of the day – which cheese would he select for our 'saddlebags' today? As we were staying at The Feathers again that night, whichever cheeses he didn't pick could have a 'day off' and stay resting in the fridge. Without any hint or inkling of his intended choice, he went downstairs and returned with the dense and fudgy Innes Log. Not only would this goat's cheese be delicious, he'd reckoned, but it made sense to eat the soft offerings first and leave the sturdier lot for later. I packed it and the crackers in my pack and would buy a few goodies from Thomas the Baker on our way. So, with our bags at the ready, we headed to breakfast.

The large dining room had a formality about it and Olaf gestured to sit at a table by the wall. The only others in the room were a couple in their mid-50s a few tables away speaking in hushed tones, so we tiptoed past them to the buffet, piled our bowls with yoghurt, cereal and fruit, then slunk back without uttering a word. For some reason, I felt like a school kid resisting the urge to laugh and when Olaf's cereal crunching broke the silence, I couldn't help myself. I snorted a giggle and it broke the quiet in the room and Olaf, in his sociable way, turned to the 'hushed' fit-looking couple.

"Looks like you're ready for a good day's walk. Where are you heading today?" he asked.

14

"Osmotherley," the English-accented woman replied.

"That's quite a walk for one day," I added, knowing we'd allowed two to get there.

"Oh yes, that *would* be a solid walk but we're starting from Sutton Bank today. A taxi is going to drop us there in about 10 minutes."

"Sounds like you're walking the Cleveland Way," Olaf said, "and you're a day ahead of us."

"Oh, right. Yes, we are," she said. "How many days are you taking?"

"Nine. And you?" Olaf asked.

"We're taking 10," the man chimed in. "Taking our time to enjoy the surrounds and have an ale or two along the way. If it was up to Sheila, we'd do it faster but I'm very happy with 10 days. Mind you, did you see some chap ran the whole thing in about 20 hours recently? Now, that's crazy."

"Gee, we're a couple of old tortoises then, aren't we?" I said. "And 'hairs' are in short supply with us." Even I cringed at my lame banter as I pointed to Olaf and my matching bald heads. "How did you find yesterday's walk? Did you go to Rievaulx Abbey and the White Horse?"

"It's a good walk. Not too strenuous and plenty of time for side trips. We enjoyed the Abbey," Sheila said, "but Andy thought the White Horse was a waste of time. Still, I'm glad we did it."

"Well, you couldn't really see it, that's all, unless you walked to the bottom," Andy said, "and I wasn't going to do that. But the walk is good, just don't expect too much from the horse. Now, they could be words to live by." We all chuckled.

"We'd better be off. Good luck with the walk," Sheila said. Her no-fuss, direct manner confirmed she held the reins, while her strong, compact body oozed a physical confidence I envied. Andy, by contrast, was tall and rangy, laid-back with an apparent willingness to go with the flow. They gathered their up-to-the-minute gear and headed for the door.

"You too," we said simultaneously, then refilled our coffee as a trickle of newly seated patrons went about their breakfast.

As I savoured the bitter brew, Sheila's assurance of a comfortable day was a relief and filled me with renewed confidence to tackle day one. It was good to start with optimism. Olaf was looking at me with a strange facial expression and I couldn't be sure, because he quickly blew his nose, but he appeared almost teary thinking about the gravity of the day. Either that or he simply needed to blow his nose and I misconstrued the moment. He was my bedrock, giving gentle yet strong support, offering calm amid my hot-headedness, challenging me from my comfort zone and loving me fully. I'd somehow managed to get through 43 years quite capably on my own but having Olaf in my life now, I had no idea how I'd ever cope without him. I can never thank our eccentric, purple-haired friend Bernadette enough for her matchmaking plan.

Bernadette was an art teacher at the same secondary college where Olaf was a sports administrator and so knew of his recent marriage breakdown. She and I had been friends since our Art History studies 10 years prior and she knew my solidly single status would only budge for somebody out of the ordinary. So, in a typical 'what is there to lose?' moment, she decided to play Cupid to see where it led.

It was a mid-winter Sunday afternoon and Bernie suggested a catch-up drink, a few laughs and an overdue natter at her place. We'd both been busy and time had slid along without a chance to see one another.

"By the way," she said on the phone following my acceptance, "I'm sure you won't mind but a workmate, actually he's a good friend, might call in later with his bathroom plans. I hope that's okay with you?"

"Yeah, of course that's fine," I said, "I'll bring cheese and wine and his bathroom will be sorted in no time. See you later on." And I didn't give it another thought. It was logical he'd want her creative advice and besides, her husband Donald had plumbing knowledge, so they were an obvious choice to brainstorm ideas. It just made sense.

I collected armfuls of goodies from my car, having brought a mountain of provisions beyond the promised cheddar and chardonnay and tried desperately not to drop anything as I walked past a pale blue Kombi parked outside Bernadette's inviting sandstone bungalow. Bernie took ages to answer the door or perhaps it seemed that way, thanks to my overflowing and awkward offerings, but when she did open up she was excited to see me.

"Soooooooooo. Are you jolly?" she shouted, using her favourite phrase, as I followed into the open-plan kitchen. "How is my gorgeous, funny and incredibly smart friend?"

"I'm very jolly, thanks," I said, finding her effusiveness odd even for her. "Been busy at work, but other than that--" I was taken aback by the presence of a man sitting at the end of the kitchen island, holding a glass of white wine, looking over what appeared to be some sort of plans.

"Hi," he said as he stood up, offering his hand and looking directly into my eyes, "I'm Olaf."

"Oh, hi," I managed, clumsily putting everything down to return his handshake and meet his gaze. His hazel-coloured eyes were kind, warm and inviting and my flushing cheeks took me straight back to adolescence.

"I hope you don't mind me crashing your happy hour. Er, assuming you're Vicki, of course."

"Oh, sorry. Sorry. Yes, that's me. I'm Vicki. Sorry." God, where was my head? "Yes, Bernie warned me about you. Oh, hang on, I didn't mean *warn*, I meant --"

He laughed, a comfortable, friendly, accepting laugh.

"I'm sure she *did* warn you about me." But she hadn't warned me, had she? She hadn't warned me her friend was going to set

17

off all sorts of unexpected chemistry, causing me to stammer like a teenager. "Or at least warn you I was going to bore you with my bathroom plans." He gestured over the drawings in front of him, then placed a colour swatch of paints on top.

"Yes, she did mention that." I was distracted again, this time by his large, caring hands and couldn't believe I was gibbering like this.

Bernadette chuckled as she handed me a glass of wine.

"Well, I mentioned the bathroom plans but didn't say a word about being boring. I swear."

"Oh, sorry. I didn't mean that," I said, "I meant she said you might --"

"Anyway, doesn't matter," she said, rescuing me. "Here's cheers!"

"Cheers!" We said, clinking glasses.

Donald joined us, refilled empty glasses and easy conversation flowed, although I continued to bumble along while losing track of time. Then Olaf had to leave for a family gathering and, as he drove off in his Kombi, Bernadette pinched my arm until he was gone, then screamed so loudly it was a miracle her windows didn't smash.

Now, a decade on from that embarrassing and exhilarating first meeting, as I again looked into Olaf's eyes across the breakfast table, a line from a Beach Boys song played in my mind's jukebox: *God only knows what I'd be without you.*

I drained my cup and we readied ourselves for our next adventure together, this time along the Cleveland Way. I hoped I wasn't going to let him down.

With our tummies full and an adventure to have, we grabbed our gear and set off. I breathed in to take in the moment as we walked past the square's symbolic Market Cross and my nostrils filled with irresistible bakery smells. Bread rolls and Scotch eggs were my selection, although there was so much to tempt me; a couple of tomatoes to complement the cheese. It was close to 10:00am, the summer sun was shining and I squeezed Olaf's hand, almost like a starting gun as we began on our way. We headed north-west past the twelfth century All Saint's Church where a large 'Cleveland Way' sign confirmed the journey had begun.

Remembering my earlier quip about being tortoises and not hares and, given the uncertainty around my physical stamina, I was happy to embrace the 'slow and steady wins the race' attitude and our pace was leisurely but steady. The birds were chirping and the verdant meadows almost glistened as we ventured up a narrow, paved track. As we left the village proper, a large, stone marker on our left etched with an acorn and names of villages we'd walk through, signalled the starting point. I knew the acorn had been the symbol for England and Wales National Trails for more than 50 years, but when I saw it carved in stone, it somehow felt like an omen. We'd be seeing it for the next 175 kilometres on the etched, wooden way-markers guiding us to Filey and, given its ancient symbolism, I knew we were on the right path (both geographically and spiritually). If mighty oaks from little acorns grow, this determined little acorn was ready to flourish.

As we took our first official steps, we were confronted and unnerved by three separate 'Missing Persons' signs posted on a giant oak tree and I speculated about their fate. Had we totally underestimated the walk or were these disappearances completely unrelated? Surely, we wouldn't suffer the same fate or get ourselves totally lost. The thought lingered, so I decided to adopt the acorn as my symbolic talisman and, with Olaf by my side, was sure we'd arrive at our destination safe and sound in nine days' time. I could dismiss any concerns and get going.

On the opposite side of the path, amid a circle of red, white and pink petunias, a much cheerier sign read, *Happy Birthday Cleveland Way. All best wishes from Helmsley Walled*

Garden for today and the next fifty years. That was more like it – an uplifting note to get us underway. I smiled at the thought we were about to humbly tread this path like many thousands in the past, whether on a personal pilgrimage, seeking an escape or healing from illness, like me. I embraced Hippocrates' description of walking as 'Man's Best Medicine' and was eager for my dose.

With the 900-year-old partial stone ruins of Helmsley Castle's east tower dominating the skyline behind, and buttercups and forget-me-nots lining the well-trodden path, we walked to the top of an incline.

"I've read about these kissing gates," I said, scurrying through the narrow, hinged contraption. "Only one person at a time can get through, then we have to kiss and then the other person is allowed through after that. So, pucker up."

"Do I have a choice?" Olaf asked, before we kissed over the wooden railing.

"Or maybe it was two kisses," I joked, but we kissed again anyway.

"Can I come through now?"

"Okay - you may." I opened the latch. "I hope there's lots of these gates, they're fun."

"I'm sure there will be. And things like stiles and snecks – such great words."

"Kissing gates are my favourite already. I'll keep my lip balm at the ready, just in case."

"Best to be prepared."

We wandered along a stone path flanked by grazing sheep, who were bleating and somehow managing to harmonise with the local birdsong to complete our peaceful soundtrack. Further on, to my delight, was another kissing gate and Olaf, quicker off the mark this time, dashed through and stood expectantly with lips at the ready. We were only a few kilometres in but I was loving the walk already.

An hour passed as we walked through woodland, on pebbly paths and alongside grazing pastures and we hadn't seen another person.

"I've got to admit, it's nice to not hear 'Buen Camino' every few minutes," Olaf said, jolting me back from an almost trance-like state.

"Such a contrast, isn't it?" I agreed. "But I guess we knew that'd be the case. No-one's even heard of the Cleveland Way, let alone walked it. Not even the Brits."

"True. But I thought we'd have seen one or two people. Clearly people *are* walking it, like that couple at breakfast, but anyway, this is much more to my liking - the Camino was way too crowded."

"'Buen Cleveland Way' doesn't quite have the same ring to it, does it? *And* it's a real mouthful. I'm glad there aren't too many people – it suits me just fine."

The Camino de Santiago de Compostela pilgrimage had fascinated me since stumbling on Shirley MacLaine's book, *The Camino: A Journey of the Spirit* in the early 2000s. Her description of various regions in Spain, the panoply of people she met and her personal struggles were so colourful and life-changing, it resonated with me as a distant, albeit unlikely, possibility. But time passed and the idea was relegated deep to the back of my mind, lying dormant and forgotten for six years. Then, out of the blue, a friend gave me, *What the Psychic told the Pilgrim*, a book by Jane Christmas. She didn't know about my fascination with the walk, so it was a total coincidence. As I turned each page, the Camino's spell became more palpable and the archived spark was reignited. I just had no idea how or if I could make it happen. So, when another sign arrived years later, it was time for action.

"That's it!" I yelled. "That *is* it!"

"What's it? What's happened?" Olaf asked.

"We're going to Spain to walk the Camino."

"Hang on. Hold fire. What on earth are you talking about?"

"Simon Reeve is walking the Camino and I can't ignore it for a third time."

"Oh, right, now it's crystal clear."

"Simon Reeve is walking the Camino," I repeated, glued to the TV. "It's another sign, I can't ignore it this time. We have to do it. Come and watch and see what you think."

"Does it really matter what I think?" But he sat down anyway to watch the BBC show. "Seems like we're going to Spain. Not sure what's brought this on, but it sounds interesting."

"I knew you'd agree."

We went to Spain in 2016 and walked the final 110 kilometres of the ancient and populous 790-kilometre Camino Frances (the most travelled route of the Camino de Santiago de Compostela) and fell in love with long-distance, multiday walks.

Now on the Cleveland Way, it was a different pilgrimage. This was personal, not so much an act of devotion but a test of my own capacity to return to a 'normal' life. I was determined that cancer and its treatment weren't going to define me and despite feeling strong, I didn't want probing questions about my motivation for doing this walk. I didn't want judgement and I certainly didn't want pity or praise. So, for now, our relative isolation suited me fine, allowing me space to heal in my own way.

Boundary walls guided and accompanied us and kept Olaf intrigued for kilometres by their age, size, simplicity and strength. We soon had to navigate large, slippery stepping-stones to cross a small, gently flowing stream which demanded my full attention, so I didn't lose my footing. Safely on the other bank, the sound of rustling in the long grass brought me to a standstill.

"What's that?" I shrieked. "Did you hear that?"

"Don't worry. It's fine. No need to be jumpy."

"Is it a snake?" I asked, remembering an encounter in Tasmania's wilderness years earlier.

We'd arrived in Cradle Mountain National Park a week before Christmas but summer temperatures were absent, barely topping 10 degrees and dropping to freezing overnight, it was hardly classic 'snake weather'. On the day we walked Dove Lake Circuit, it was crisp and the vibrant sky and deep blue lake were separated by golden vegetation and imposing, jagged outcrops, as we walked along the flat, board-walked track, absorbed in nature's gifts.

"STOP!" yelled Olaf. "Stay completely still."

"What's the matter?" I asked, not sure what to expect.

"Up there – can't you see it? A snake. A big one, all curled up. It looks to have stripes, I think, so could be a tiger snake."

"Oh God, they're really poisonous, aren't they? What do we do?"

"Stay still, I guess, or I'm happy to turn back. We can't keep going, so let's leave it to enjoy the sun."

"Come on, let's go! I'm keen to skedaddle."

But as we turned to backtrack, the snake must've finished sun-bathing, uncoiling itself before slithering into the thick, yellow shrubbery lining both sides of the path. We stood holding our breath until we were certain it was gone, then scurried past that spot, delighted we could continue, albeit with an elevated heart rate and heightened vigilance.

I hadn't expected encounters like that in England, but it *was* a warm day and any self-respecting snake should be out in the sunshine.

"What do you reckon - one of those venomous Yorkshire yellow-bellies?" Olaf asked.

"Not funny. I'm sure they have snakes here, don't they? Obviously, not as deadly as ours, but they *must* have them here," I said.

"I'm not sure, to be honest." We kept walking, Olaf slightly ahead as I followed nervously. Barely able to contain his laughter,

23

he added, "They must have adders around the place somewhere – presumably black ones."

It took me a while to cotton on.

"Oh, black adders. You goose. Well then, to quote *Blackadder*, I hope you have 'a cunning plan' if it actually is a snake."

"I'm pretty sure it's *not* a snake. More likely a pheasant or partridge or one of those things they like to hunt around here."

"Oh right. So, good news is, it's not a snake. But the bad news is, there could be the odd, stray hunting bullet. Great!"

"Relax! Let's enjoy ourselves in these beautiful surrounds. We're going well, so let's settle in and, as they say, 'mind how we go'."

From the corner of my eye, I caught a glimpse of a white, bobbing tail scampering into the undergrowth, presumably the hare responsible for the rustling. At least, I hoped so. As for Olaf's attempted humour - I had no explanation for that.

We walked in a comfortable rhythm, Olaf five steps ahead in his 'lucky' blue shirt, along a foot-worn path, over a vehicle track when a stone building on the right demanded our attention. It was Griff Lodge, a stone gatehouse behind a small picket fence, with gorgeous lunette windows and a formidable presence. We were so distracted by its form and discovering it was mentioned in the Domesday Book that we almost missed what was to our left, an opening in the pine woodland offering glimpses over the Rye valley's lush farmland. We descended once more through woodland before arriving at a T-junction. Our guidebook instructed us left past a stone cottage and along a hedge-lined road shared with intermittent traffic.

"There's Rievaulx Abbey," Olaf said, catching sight of the former Cistercian monastery. "The turnoff can't be too far."

"Where? I can't see it." I swivelled to look around.

"Over there, short-arse." He pointed over a tall hedge.

"Hey! I'm not that short; I'm just not a giraffe like you. Anyway, I'll see it soon enough."

"No, you're more of an emu, I guess. But the good news is, we're almost there."

He was right. Only moments later we were at the abbey's turnoff and, although this side trip would add to the day's kilometres, we really wanted to do it. Part of the joy of walking lay in its diversions, seeing where you ended up and what you'd find along the way. If it meant I was exhausted at the end of the day, that was a risk I was willing to take. There was still a long way to go, but right now I was feeling good and ready to turn off.

We took the right turn with the River Rye emanating a soothing burble to our left. Sheep were in the clover-covered paddocks opposite, dotted around Rye House; it was a grand entry to the 12th century monastic remains, even in the 21st century. As the vista towards the Gothic ruins opened up, the grandeur and presence of what remained were truly awesome. As we neared, a sense of how the 650-or-so monks lived self-sufficiently became clearer until Henry VIII put an end to its 400-year existence by dissolving England's monasteries in 1538.

"Oh. My. Word," I said. "Now, *that* is impressive."

"It's huge. Imagine what it was like in its heyday. I wonder how they built it and how long it took." Olaf always wondered about these sorts of things.

"It must've been an idyllic life, although, I guess, heating would've been an issue."

"It *did* have walls back then," he smirked.

"Of course it had walls, but it still would've been freezing in winter."

"True. Maybe they drank enough of their wine to keep warm, a bit like the Jesuits at Sevenhill in the Clare Valley."

"If that was the case, they *did* have the idyllic set-up. I reckon I'd have almost signed up for that."

"Right. I'd sign up for a decent coffee right now. Let's hope the café can deliver."

I was ready for our first break, despite having only walked an hour. It was day one with a lot of kilometres ahead and another eight days to get through, so it was important to pace myself.

The contemporary National Trust café sat in the abbey's grounds, 50 metres from the light grey stone edifice and satisfied our desire for coffee, with the addition of delicious home-made biscuits. We sat at an outdoor table in dappled light penetrating the canopy of beech and oak trees, looking at the remains of the former centre of monasticism in Britain and took in the magnitude of the moment. The abbey appeared to be shrouded in an ethereal misty veil, but the day was clear and there was no obvious reason for the mysterious optical haze. Perhaps it was a trick of the eye or maybe, glimmering auras from spirits past, but whichever the case, I was glad we'd taken this side trip.

After half an hour or so, we needed to get going, gather our packs and ready ourselves to get back on the path. As I bent down to pick up my walking pole, a dozen or so acorns caught my eye, scattered under our table. It was unseasonal for acorns to drop in July, so was this another omen, a spiritual nod and wink that I was on the right track, that I would grow and flourish along this path? I quickly refocused as Olaf handed me my jacket, then prodded me with his walking pole as we had to get cracking.

My muscles had tightened from the break and took five or so minutes to warm up as we retraced our steps back to the turn off. Reset and back on the right path, we strode across the ancient, arched, limestone bridge and slotted smoothly into our rhythm with Olaf slightly ahead. The aural accompaniment to the crunch of our footsteps was the rural soundscape of barking dogs, distant bellowing cows, birds chirping loudly and the occasional croaking frog. This was seriously good for my soul.

Past ponds, along hedged paths, over more slippery stepping-stones and past an out-of-place log cabin, which would be more at home in the Bavarian Alps than on the Yorkshire Moors. It might have been a warning sign that the gradient was about to significantly increase, not to the extent of the Alps, but enough to induce huff and puff as we climbed the Hambleton Hills towards the village of Cold Kirby.

As we stopped for some water near St Michael's Church, I did a quick, almost subconscious check-in with my body. I was going okay, but with focused consideration, there may have been a small hot spot developing on my left big toe. Every walker knows the importance of looking after their feet and mine were now of particular concern. I had neuropathy or nerve damage in my toes, like a sharp version of pins and needles oddly combined with a general numbness. It would come and go on its own terms. And I was concerned about my toenails, which were soft and chalky and vulnerable to possibly dropping off at some stage on this walk. Should I check on my precarious feet now or wait until we'd finished the day's walk? We'd covered roughly 10 kilometres and still had about six to go – or even more if we took the spur off to the White Horse of Kilburn – a chalky figure cut into the side of a hill covering 6,500 square metres. I decided I'd check the state of my feet later; I had to stop being paranoid about every little niggle, nag and sting. But I was more tired than I'd expected as I replayed the assuring advice we received at breakfast in my mind - *It's a lovely walk. Not too strenuous and plenty of time for those side trips.* And it *was* lovely and not too strenuous to this point, yet I still felt slightly heavy in my stride. I worried if this was a so-called 'easy' day, how would I cope with the notoriously difficult section I'd read about – Osmotherley to Clay Bank - in two days' time?

I snapped myself out of that mindset, otherwise we wouldn't even finish day one if I thought too hard about all my aches and pains. It was a case of putting one foot in front of the other and remembering the invaluable advice I'd received - just focus on what *IS* and not on what *IF*. So, with that in mind, I repacked my water bottle, nodded to Olaf that it was time to move on and listened to the skylarks singing.

A little further on was another kissing gate and Olaf dashed through with childlike fervour, quickly shutting it and leaning across with a cheeky grin. I kissed his cheek but was denied entry. I kissed him on the nose but again no entry. For my third effort, I kissed his lips and this time he relented, so I weaved through the contraption to the other side.

"We'll need to pick up our pace if we're going to see this White Horse," Olaf said.

"Why, what's the time?"

"Almost 2:30pm. We're going okay but we haven't had lunch yet and we've got to be at the visitor centre by 5."

"Right. How far is there to go?"

"We've walked almost 12 kilometres, so if we do the side trip, it's roughly six and a half more."

"And if we don't do it?"

"About three. What do you think? Are you feeling okay?"

"Let me see – that gives us two and a half hours to have lunch, walk six and a half ks, and be at Sutton Bank for the taxi at 5pm? Sounds doable." So much for having plenty of time for stops along the way.

A taxi had been arranged to take us back to Helmsley, a time pressure I didn't want or need. Still, we *could* choose not to walk the extra kilometres or we could slot into our walking rhythm and get on with it. So, with a nod and a double pat on Olaf's backside, we set off and within seconds, I was looking at his blue-shirted back and laden pack.

A long, but gentle, climb did nothing to assist our speed and I became agitated with my legs as they refused to move any faster. A weight had arrived in my thighs and seemed to have settled in for the duration. I pondered changing my mind and scrapping the side trip, after all, it was said to be a waste of time, according to Andy. What if he was right and we'd expended valuable energy? As I looked ahead for Olaf to suggest we forget it, his familiar stride was nowhere to be seen.

He'd already turned left toward the forestry plantation and was motoring ahead, keen to meet the deadline *and* see the horse. When I took the turn, he was about 20 metres ahead, oblivious to my lagging energy reserves and stubbornly weighty legs. I shouted out and he immediately turned, surprised to see how far I'd fallen behind; I caught up, had a split-second breather, before he set off again, a little too quickly for my liking.

The path led us through a horse training track of white rails and stables, but not a horse, nor person, were anywhere to be seen. It felt like we were trespassing but our trail was clearly marked and we *were* on the right track, fittingly, a horse track. We tiptoed through the property without speaking a word; it was a strange experience, like we were on an abandoned movie set even though it was a working farm.

The midsummer sunshine enveloped us as we headed towards Sutton Bank and having only seen a handful of people all day, we now had to have our wits about us to cross the busy A170. Dozens of cars whizzed by and after what seemed like ages, we scampered across and headed uphill along a forestry firebreak. Past a stand of silver birch, we reached a T-junction and it was time to make the decision – did we go left and walk the extra 3.2 kilometres, or go right and enjoy a coffee or ice-cream soon? We hadn't had lunch yet and breakfast and snacks had well and truly worn off. I was definitely leaning towards turning right, enjoying our lunch with that coffee and taking all the time pressure off. Plus, I could check my feet which were a nagging worry.

Without consultation, Olaf chose left, so I followed muttering in annoyance.

"Okay, so we're definitely doing it," I sniped. "Would've been nice to have had a say in it."

"First of all – we're not *definitely* doing anything. And secondly, if we didn't come this way, we wouldn't have found this - the perfect spot for lunch."

Having emerged through the thicket, a panoramic view over the green miscellany of countryside opened out as we stood on the brow of Sutton Bank. I'd read that author James Herriot had described it as one of the finest views in England, and he was right. To think, my near tantrum almost denied us the chance to enjoy it. Thankfully, Olaf knew to ignore my bottom lip-quivering antics and push on, I had to acknowledge that, so we stopped to have lunch and enjoy the break. It was a relief to take off our packs and indulge in the first of our cheeses, complemented by all the accompaniments, of course. We sat on a provided seat, unpacked the goodies and I praised Olaf's choice of the Innes Log. We'd have to be a bit strategic in our cheese choices in days to come, but today he'd nailed it – the bright, zingy, hazelnutty flavour was a taste sensation.

For almost half an hour we peered over a sea of greenery, ate, took photos and tried to absorb the tranquillity. But the sounds of nature couldn't compete with the traffic noise rising from the busy road below, along with those from the Yorkshire Gliding Club nearby, but we still embraced the moment and I let my muscles rest.

Buoyed by the break and sustained by the cheese, my enthusiasm for the side trip returned and we walked in the opposite direction to our day's final destination along a well-graded path. With productive farmland to our left, we skirted along the edge of Rouston Scar's escarpment and stopped for a few moments to watch gliders take-off and land right beside us. After about one and a half kilometres, we reached the site of the hillside figure. But despite its size, it was hard to see. From where we stood, it looked like an unremarkable white rock surface which could've been anything.

"Andy was right," I said, "it's a bit of a waste of time."

"I thought he might've been overstating it, but yep, there's not a lot to see here," Olaf said, looking around in case we'd missed something.

"There's a sign over here. Oh, this is where it tells us it's best viewed from a distance or from the car park down there."

"Do you want to go down to see this thing?"

"In a word – no. It's got to be close to a kilometre down and then back up. And we've got another one and a half kilometres back to that T-junction. So, no. I do *not* want to go down to the car park. The only car park I'm keen to see is the one we need to get to by 5pm."

"Okay. You've made your thoughts clear – let's start heading back. At least we know the views will be specky."

"The finest view in England, apparently."

"Thank you, Mr Herriot."

"My pleasure. I wonder what he would've made of the White Horse."

"Well, I'm sure he's written about it somewhere. But you know what's funny?"

"What?"

"It's not until you're standing right on top of it that you're told it's best viewed from a distance."

"Ha! Someone had a sense of humour or a sense of irony."

"Yeah, well, we'd better get a wriggle on."

And so, we retraced our steps along what felt like the longest stretch of path known to man, my muscles becoming more and more weary and my mind in sync with my muscles. Gliders came and went around us and we arrived back at our picnic spot about an hour after we'd packed it away. I trudged on until we arrived back at the T-junction, this time going straight on, tired and eager to arrive at the Sutton Bank National Park Visitors Centre.

As day one's walk neared its end, a day which was a long time coming, the last few hundred metres seemed to take forever. Today had taken longer than expected, thanks to my hard-to-get-moving legs, a couple of longish breaks and two significant side trips along the way. But we still hadn't finished and my leaden body needed to keep going, keep pushing, for the short distance left.

I was surprised and disoriented to encounter the A170 again; my bearings were completely out and I had no idea which direction was which. I panicked that we might've somehow doubled back and, right at the finish, were lost. I grabbed the guidebook, which confirmed we *had* to be on the right path and, besides, we'd put our faith in the guiding acorns, not only on the way-markers, but also on the oaks all day and there was no denying them. So, we crossed back over the A170, with far less traffic this time and I wanted to yell - *are we there yet?* But having already had an earlier mini tantrum, I refrained and, as we squeezed between two timber posts leading to a picnic area, the visitors centre appeared among the trees and we were there. Thank goodness, exactly where we needed to be and slightly ahead of schedule. Olaf suggested an ice-cream, so who was I to disagree?

The taxi arrived and, in reverse of our morning drop-off, we packed our gear into the boot and secured ourselves for the short drive. The anticipation of a hot shower grew as we neared the town and I could almost feel the day's toil already washing away but I also had fears for my feet. Would that hot spot I'd felt, growing over the day's trek, be okay or could it jettison future days? And had we overdone it first up by taking those two 'extra' trips, making it closer to 20 kilometres than 16? All I knew was I was very sweaty, very tired and very relieved that we'd managed this part of the task but there was still a long way to go.

We arrived at the hotel and slowly, very slowly, grabbed our gear and ambled upstairs to our room.

"I'm almost too scared to take off my shoes," I said.

"I'm a bit scared about that too, but probably for different reasons," Olaf said.

"Ha, ha, ha! Okay, they'll probably be pongy, but it's my toes – I don't know what state they'll be in."

"Only one way to find out. Whip them off and let's have a look."

"Right-o. Here goes."

As I bent to undo my laces, I was sure I heard my muscles yell to hurry up and get in the shower as they'd tightened up and were seeking some attention of their own. As I yanked the shoes off, my feet were elated at escaping their confinement, then overjoyed when the socks were peeled off and my toes wriggled in their new freedom. My eyes darted towards my big left toe where a small red spot looked angry but not blistered – yet. I might be able to manage it with proper taping and care for the remaining days. Now for the toenails, how had they coped? An individual assessment of each returned excellent results: no damage and all intact. This was as good a result as I could've hoped for on day one as my feet had survived, but there was still the worry about my stamina and fitness. We were only a fraction of the way there - 20 kilometres down, around 160 to go.

Then fantasy became reality for my aching body as a hot shower removed all traces of sweat, grime and some of the fatigue. Olaf busied himself, handwashing his now-favourite shirt and a few items, just to keep on top of the laundry, with the heated towel rail proving an excellent drying device. He then revelled in the joys of a shower and, shortly after, we headed downstairs for a well-earned drink in the bar. Like a repeat of the previous evening, Olaf bought drinks and I scored an outside table with a great view over the busy market square. I sat in a satisfied, semi-exhausted numbness that comes after physical exertion and watched locals and tourists heading out for dinner. I was gazing into space waiting for Olaf to return when I noticed small carvings around the windowsills, on the tables, and the same motif running along the bar. The more I looked, the more I couldn't believe it, there were wood-carved mice and I hadn't noticed them until now.

A now-traditional bag of crisps accompanied our pint

before we headed to the trattoria for more delicious, energy-laden carbs, which we ate with less haste this time. Back in our room, Olaf was keen to make sure his fast-drying shirt lived up to its promise and his excited smile, akin to having won a raffle, told me it had. I was tired and ready for bed but also wanted to be organised again for the morning.

"I forgot we still had this in here," I said pulling out the half-eaten Innes Log. "This probably doesn't qualify as *treating it right*.'"

"It'll be okay. I'll whack it in the fridge. Do you think you'll want it again tomorrow?"

"Let's try one of the others. Maybe the Coolea – what do you reckon? And do the same as we did today with a few things from Thomas?"

"Perfect. I'll take this down now. Which one is the Coolea?"

"The wax-covered one. And let's have the quince paste too. Geez, we'll be quite the affineurs by the time we've finished."

"Well, let's see how we go before you start professing expertise. Don't get ahead of yourself."

Olaf found the kitchen in darkness but was thankful the door was still unlocked. He returned the day's uneaten cheese to the stash in the fridge, then hurried out again. He returned to our room, grinning and emanating a lightness of spirit and life. He was happy.

"I actually felt like a thief doing that little foray, even though it's *our* cheese," he said.

"Cheese sorted. Now, we'd better get our other luggage ready."

Our luggage was to be collected at 8:00am SHARP or it would miss the transfer to our next accommodation. Neither of us fancied carrying those cases the 18.5 kilometres ahead, so we got that ready first then focused on our packs. I flopped on the bed and stared at the ceiling.

"Well, we made it through day one," I said. "We actually made it through day one."

Olaf lay next to me. "We sure did. I'd even say we blitzed it."

"Mmmmm. I'm not sure about that. I'm too exhausted to feel like we blitzed it. This is going to sound dumb but today doesn't even feel real. I mean, obviously it's real because my feet are telling me so, but we're here and we're doing this and we've made it over the first hurdle."

"Hey," Olaf grabbed my hand, "it's real alright. You were awesome today and you'll be awesome for the next eight days."

"Now who's getting ahead of themselves? I'm going to take it one day at a time but I got through today and I'm so proud, if that's the right word. I know walking 20kms isn't earth-shattering or anything, but it's been such a struggle to get here and I'm -"

"Shhhhh," Olaf wrapped his arms around me, "you have every right to feel proud of yourself and every right to be exhausted. Day one conquered. I knew we'd get here. I guess you being so stubborn is finally a good thing!"

"Watch it! And look who's calling *me* stubborn. I just feel lucky I had this walk to focus on and strive for and, if that makes me stubborn, I'll gladly wear that."

EVEN LONGER 24 HOURS

Heading to the appointment I felt calm and controlled, almost positive I'd somehow misconstrued the GP's words and things weren't as bad as they initially seemed. The surgeon would surely put a better perspective on things and, although it looked like I had breast cancer, surely, he'd have a straightforward solution. Perhaps a lumpectomy, then radiation or radiation on its own and I'd read about successful trials with medication. Of course, it was going to be tough. All of those options were confronting but I'd find a way to get through. Other thoughts zinged around like a pinball machine, like being able to keep working with a few minor adjustments and life could continue with minimal disruption. Whatever lay ahead, I'd fit it into my world, not let it overtake my life and resist letting it define me.

I'd been so caught up in this self-dialogue, I hadn't noticed Olaf's silence and was shocked to see the fearful expression set into his usually untroubled face. His capacity to say just the right thing, break the ice with a quip or calm me down with logic, could be relied on to make things better, but he was lost in thought too as we travelled.

The blank-faced receptionist handed over a sea of paperwork to complete, instructed us to sit and wait until we were called, all without a skerrick of eye contact. When someone called my name, everything ramped up. My heart beat so fast and strong, I thought it might burst through my chest and my breathing was shallow and rapid to the point of almost panting. We entered the surgeon's small, windowless office - an examination bed against one wall, another lined with patient files - and were offered a seat across a messy, paper-strewn desk. He had a warmth about his manner, despite his gruff voice and he leant forward on his elbows with a pen in his right hand. I held my breath and my stomach did backflips as he peered over his glasses perched on his nose, cleared his throat and delivered the words like a punch to my solar plexus.

"You can see two sizeable cancers in your right breast," he said, pointing to my scans mounted on a lightbox. "Grade 3." His pen making virtual circles around the obvious masses on display. "You'll need a mastectomy, then chemotherapy, probably for six months."

"Fuck! FUCK!" It was all I could manage.

My mind went into a tailspin of a million thoughts but I couldn't even formulate one. It was like a helicopter blade was whirring in my head, winding up to top throttle. Chaos and confusion washed over me as I sat in a foggy, numb haze, the room hot and claustrophobic. The surgeon's mouth continued to move but I couldn't hear a thing above the deafening noise in my head. I just wanted to run, get out of that office and gasp some fresh air, but my body was frozen, glued to the chair like a statue and I started to cry. And once I'd started, I couldn't stop. I didn't want to stop – it felt good to release the anxiety and worry – so the tears flowed unabashed. There was no place for restraint and control and abandoning it felt right. Besides, I had no energy, nor the capacity, to compose myself and that helicopter was persisting with its constant buzzing.

Knowing I was in my own world of emotional turmoil and, having seen it so many times before, the doctor directed his conversation to Olaf whose face had a ghostly pallor and was slightly distorted as he tried to take it all in. Then amongst the turbulence, I had one urgent thought:

"Our holiday to the UK next July, will we still be able to go?"

"Um, well, I would think so," he said, taken aback. "That's what, nine months away? I imagine that should be fine."

"We're doing a 175-kilometre walk, along the Cleveland Way," Olaf said. "Is that still possible, do you think?"

"I'm wondering why the hell you'd want to spoil a good holiday like that," he said with a smile, "but yes, you've got time. You're fit and, assuming all goes smoothly, you should be fine. I reckon you might surprise yourself how well you'll come through all this."

Surgery was booked for late Friday afternoon, the last surgery of the week and, in a strange twist, I now couldn't wait. I'd seen photos of mastectomy scars, read stories of grief and loss but, apart from an overwhelming sadness, my simple thought was if the breast was gone, the cancers were gone. I could focus on treatment and get on with life. So, in the only way I knew, I embraced the idea of surgery and became impatient for it.

Olaf was by my side as we waited for the allotted time. He did his best to keep me buoyed and distracted and we even managed a few laughs, but the uncertainty of what lay ahead meant there were large chunks of silence and occasionally my emotions would bubble up through tears.

"I'm just so sad," I said, "and I'm sorry to put you through it all."

"That's ridiculous. We're in this together and we'll get through it," Olaf said, "and I'm sad too. It's shit. But you're going to be fine." He grabbed my hand.

"I know, I just feel so guilty that I'm dragging you through this. It might sound stupid but it's how I feel. I can't help it."

"Well, you can stop it right now. I love you. Okay? Love. Love. Love." He kissed my forehead.

"Oh God! Now I'm really blubbering. I love you so much. I don't know how I'd do any of this without you."

"Well, you don't have to. I'm with you every step of the way."

The wall clock in the recovery room was the first thing I noticed. It was early evening now and I was desperately thirsty. My next thought was that the outside world hadn't changed while my world was being reshaped; nurses went about their business, checking charts, blood pressures and temperatures and offering desired water to dehydrated patients.

"Here you go, Sweetie," a nurse said handing me a small paper cup. "Just sip it slowly to wet your whistle and we'll see how that settles."

"Did everything go okay?" I asked, my voice croaky and faint.

"Smooth as silk, love. The doctor will be along in a jiffy and he'll have all the answers but no need to worry. All went well, I believe."

"That's good. It's just later than I thought, so did it take longer than it should?"

She leaned in close and whispered, "Just between you and me, the doctors took a tea break before they started your surgery, so you got bumped for a cuppa. Only 30 minutes or so but at least it meant they were spritely for you."

"Oh, okay. Well, I'm glad they weren't tired. Or grumpy. Or both." My eyelids closed and it felt good. I let go of any attempt to keep chatting and sunk back into a pleasant, drug-altered semiconsciousness.

My bed whizzed through corridors, in and out of lifts, flung open doors and spun around into the luxurious room I'd managed to score. It was big enough to house six patients, but I had it all to myself, with a floor-to-ceiling window overlooking parklands and a lounge setting arranged to enjoy the view. Olaf was doing just that but was instantly by my side as the bed was manoeuvred into place. He gently kissed my forehead just as the surgeon made his grand entrance.

"Well then," he said, peering over his glasses, "how's the patient feeling?" He didn't wait for a reply and was fidgeting with a tube emanating from my right side. "All went well. Now, this here is a drain. It'll annoy you but we've got to get rid of that fluid. Anyway, I'll pop in, in the morning, when we'll have a closer look at everything, so get a good sleep and I'll see you tomorrow." He nodded at Olaf and was on his way.

"I feel really tired," I said to Olaf as I shut my eyes.

He again kissed my forehead and whispered something I didn't quite catch, then left me to sleep with the promise to return in the morning with a strong, long black coffee, the perfect brew to fortify me for what lay ahead.

It didn't look like I thought it would when the bandage was peeled away. Those photos had shown patients with completely flat chests, no evidence a breast ever existed, just a scar and that's it. But *my* mastectomy didn't look like that at all. I had a lot of skin at either end of the 18-centimetre vibrant cut, under my armpit and in the cleavage, and figured it was post-surgery swelling, but it was there in case I chose a reconstruction. And above the incision was a concave crater where breast tissue once sat, about 10 centimetres below my collarbone with the pectoral muscle underneath.

It was a big shock at first, not at all how I'd pictured it, but that quickly returned to relief knowing the cancers were now gone. I would adjust to my changed body as I'd done four years earlier after an urgent hysterectomy, thanks to adenomyosis - an excruciating and debilitating disease. That surgery had stamped me with a bulbous scar, running 13-centimetres from my bellybutton downwards. I went through a kind of grieving then, not for the loss of perceived womanhood, I was past that reproduction window and had Olaf's two adult children in my life, with the hope of becoming a grandma at some stage. It was a grief that my body couldn't fix itself; it had pathologically let me down. And here I was again in the same space but this time, although I was deeply sad, I knew I had the strength to cope. And I'd need every bit of it.

My new lopsidedness took some adjusting to. Where there was once a weighty breast was now a void, making rolling over in bed tricky. But soon enough I adapted to the imbalance, thanks to a soft, gel-filled breast form which I placed in a mastectomy bra. It evened things up in terms of weight and aesthetics and provided an unassuming appearance under most of my clothes. Only plunging necklines were no longer possible to wear, although I'd never been a low-cut, cleavage showing person anyway.

I healed quickly over the following weeks, but my patience was regularly tested by a seroma – a typical side effect of surgery – where fluid continually pooled beneath my scar. It felt like an army of ants was marching underneath my skin as the liquid naturally moved and the only fix was a fine needle syringing a couple of times a week. It took eight weeks for the unpleasantness to stop and brought a celebrated end to those quick, lunchtime dashes to the surgeon's office.

So, I'd come through the first part of my surgeon's initial pronouncement: *You'll need a mastectomy,* healing quickly and feeling healthy. If I only had to contend with that, it would've been done and dealt with, but it was the next part of his statement that really scared me: *Then chemotherapy, probably for six months.* It was a big, frightening unknown but was sure to be a gruelling six months.

41

A GRUELLING SIX MONTHS

Nervous doesn't come close to describe how I felt as we walked into the oncologist's office for the late morning appointment in early November. Terrified was *much* closer. Whatever you call it, I felt bilious. The dozen or so 'thank you' cards lining his windowsill were a welcome sight and the meticulously ordered bookcase, which filled one wall, had one shelf, I noted amid my anxious mindset, dedicated to books about wine. On another day, we could compare notes on a favourite grape variety, region or label but today was not that day. But along with the fear, I was also impatient to get chemo started – the sooner it started, the sooner it finished and I could get back to a normal life.

Olaf's large, assuring hand squeezed mine as we sat across the neat, organised desk of the small-statured man who I hoped held all the answers. His subcontinental accent was light and he was softly spoken, at times so soft he was almost inaudible. He had kind, caring eyes and a calmness which eased the magnitude of the moment. He'd done this hundreds of times but for us it was all new and he fully respected that. The immediate outlook was optimistic, he said and for the first time in weeks I was able to relax.

"We'll start with four treatments, three weeks apart," he said, "then the second round of 12 weekly treatments. Sixteen sessions, all up over 24 weeks. But we may need to alter things along the way for one reason or another."

"So, that's about six months," Olaf said. I was glad he could focus as there were too many numbers for me to take in.

"If all goes okay. It'll depend on how Vicki reacts. We can pause for a week or so if we need to, then start up again. We can see how it goes."

"We won't be pausing," I said, a bit too forcefully. "We're going to the UK in July, so it has to be finished by then."

"Well, it's good to have a goal. Let's just see how you go." His volume louder and message clear.

"So, when can we get started?" I asked, hoping Olaf was paying attention.

"Well, we can start straight away. This afternoon if you want."

"Oh, right," I said, "the sooner we start, the better." But despite my brave exterior, I instantly felt sick and my eyes pooled with tears. So many emotions swelled but fear was winning out.

"I'll have to sort a few things out, but we can get started in a couple of hours," he said. "Go and have something to eat and come back at 1:30pm."

Food had been the last thing on my mind but now I was ravenous and craved a mountain of steaming dumplings. If this was the last meal I could taste or desire, given chemo's notorious side effects, I'd be happy.

"At least we know what's ahead now, timewise," Olaf said, seated at our favourite Chinatown restaurant, "and starting today means finishing mid-May. That's six weeks before we're due in Yorkshire."

"Plenty of time," I said with false confidence.

"Look, I need to say this - we can put the trip on hold. Maybe it's the smart thing to do anyway and see how things go. There's no point getting stressed or upset and it takes the pressure off."

43

I finished my chillied-up mouthful. "I will be walking the Cleveland Way in July, come hell or highwater."

And as the words left my mouth, it hit me that the next six months could *actually* be hell and tears of fear flowed. I knew it was okay to be frightened but I also desperately wanted to stay positive, so I harked back to my surgeon's encouraging words: *You might surprise yourself how well you'll come through all this.* I really hoped I could surprise myself.

The time arrived and a cannula was inserted in the back of my left hand after several attempts to secure a begrudging vein. A frustrated, unhelpful nurse lashed out suggesting, "You should have a port anyway!"

I had no idea what she was talking about but discovered it's a large device implanted under the skin near the collarbone which simplifies the extraction of blood and infusion of drugs for the duration of treatment. There was no way I would have one, despite heavy and constant pressure from medical staff. Yes, it would eliminate the recurring difficulties with the cannula every treatment but it seemed invasive and a constant, plastic reminder in my body. It wasn't going to happen.

With the cannula eventually in and bloods taken, I headed to the dreaded chair ready for action. I'd seen footage of cancer rooms - chairs lined up, copious bottles of hand sanitiser and bald-headed people plugged in to a myriad of drips, but reality added the smell of antiseptic, a cacophony of beeping noises and the occasional moan from a patient to add to the experience. It was vaguely familiar and yet completely foreign and, as I took my assigned chair, I felt stripped of energy, devoid of any buoyancy, resigned to this new reality. And it was *very* real.

First up: Doxorubicin, known as the 'Red Devil', thanks to its bright, red colour and side-effect inducing potency, which I could feel pumping through my vein. It continued its circuit and tears started cascading down my cheeks as the gravity of the situation hit. My vision became blurred and, as I blinked and wiped, everything remained fuzzy, even with glasses on. I was exhausted, gave up any resistance and simply shut my eyes. Another drug, Cyclophosphamide, would follow once the devil was done and, with around 1.5 hours to complete both, a doze was probably a good thing. I opened my eyes after about 30 minutes and clearly saw Olaf at the afternoon tea trolley. It offered cakes, biscuits, sandwiches, but he chose tasty cheese and crackers which became our standard snack for the next 24 weeks. It was a tiny bit of light amid the bleakness, while my taste buds still worked anyway. Yep, I must've been a mouse in a previous life.

After a big, big day, I crossed off my first dose of chemotherapy – only 15 more to go. Feeling light-headed and exhausted, we retreated home and I waited to see what happened next, a bucket within reach just in case. But it was an overwhelming lethargy which took hold and I went to bed not knowing what to expect. It was a fitful night of sweating – reeking a metallic stench – body shakes, pins and needles, a gripping headache and nausea. I slid in and out of sleep and when morning proper came, I was doing a body check-in as Olaf woke.

"How're you feeling?" he asked.

"Urgh. My legs feel as heavy as lead, actually more like full of cement. I don't know if I can even get up to go to the loo. And my voice is quivering."

"Do you feel sick?"

"A little bit. Not too bad though. But I've got no energy."

"Well, take it easy till your mum gets here. What time is she likely to arrive?"

"8:30 I think, with vanilla slices. We can save you one for later."

"Nah, no need. They're not my favourite," he laughed, got up and headed for the shower.

For the next six months, I had my Friday afternoon sessions with Olaf by my side, but work meant he was away from home all-day Saturday and couldn't look after me the day after treatment. So, my mother vowed to visit and keep me company, to continue the nurturing role she'd relished for over half a century.

Mum, a healthy 78-year-old, was the hub of the family - open-armed, family focused, warm and kind. She's smart, pragmatic, gets stuff done without fuss or recognition and is the understated and undisputed matriarch. Dad, a very active 80-year-old, is charismatic, engaging and loves to tell a story, is emotional and sensitive, gentle and loving. They've been married for 59 years and my older brother, sister and I knew we won the jackpot scoring them as our parents, enjoying a happy, uncomplicated childhood in regional South Australia. Of course, we each had our 'growing up' battles as every family does, like breaking night-time party curfews and getting sprung in a café wagging class, but being the youngest child, I knew I had it smoother, thanks to my trail-blazing siblings.

"How are you feeling, Love?" asked Mum, gently kissing my cheek, her hands loaded with paper bags filled with bakery goodies. "You're looking alright. How'd you get on?"

"I feel weird and a little bit sick, but not too bad I guess." I turned towards the kitchen but my legs refused to budge. "These things do not want to move. It's ridiculous how heavy they are."

"Well, take your time. There's no rush to be anywhere. Do you need me to help?" She'd offloaded her handful and was back by my side, her arm firmly around my shoulders.

"Nah. They're moving a bit now. I just need to fully focus to get them going but I feel a bit like a robot."

"You don't look like one." Her arm still encased me in more of a hug than for guidance and remained until I'd made it to a chair. "Your father sends his love and I've got to tell you he isn't happy about missing a vanilla slice. I'm sure you can imagine. He should be able to come next time, though."

"That's fine. I'm not sure I'm great company anyway, so he's not missing much on that front."

"Well, I don't mind if you sleep all day, darling. I'll just potter around. I brought a book and a few crosswords, but if you need anything, I'm right here."

"I'm glad you came prepared. Now, let's tuck in while they're still fresh."

"Let's. And while you're still fresh too." She slid the treat from the bag, the slab of yellow custard wobbling amid the pastry, placed it on a plate and carefully cut it in two.

We enjoyed this routine of Mum sourcing vanilla slices from a different bakery each week and then pretending to do a 'cooking show' type of judging. It was frivolous and fun but in its own way helped us both – giving me something to look forward to and giving her a sense of 'doing' something. I never had the heart to tell her vanilla slices weren't *my* favourite either.

As chemo continued, patterns emerged with the side effects which, with their predictability, offered a tiny sense of control. I knew which post-treatment days were my worst, so tried to manage life around that. I struggled with constant mild nausea, persistent concrete-laden legs, had a steady, dull headache, frustrating brain fog, regular hot flushes and interrupted sleep. Then randomly but frequently, my tongue would feel as though it was burnt, I became overly teary, had a tender stomach, and my skin took on a yellowish tinge. Bigger symptoms included moving teeth, which was off-putting when they occasionally moved as I ate, ongoing painful nerve damage in my feet and the slow deterioration of my nails – both toes and fingers – with the likelihood they would drop off.

But the most visual and obvious side effect would be losing

my hair, the outward signal to the world of my cancer and the thing to impact most on my confidence and self-esteem. At the beginning of chemo, I was offered cold cap therapy - a high-tech contraption attached like a cap which freezes your scalp during treatment. In theory it 'could' minimise hair loss but with mixed results and no guarantee of success, plus an extra hour at each session. It was an easy decision for me to make. No thank you.

It happened three weeks after that first Friday session with clumps of loose hair on my pillow. I knew it was going to happen, but it was still confronting to accept. And when those clumps started coming out in my hand, I decided to take action to avoid looking like a moth-eaten coat. Olaf plugged in the hair clippers and, when I gave him the go-ahead, he carefully and lovingly shaved my head. I tried to be brave and thought I'd prepared for this moment as best I could, but when my remaining bottle-blonde wisps hit the ground, so did my tears.

"I never thought *you'd* be shaving *my* head," I said, having often given Olaf a neatening trim.

"No. Me either." The clippers continued vibrating across my scalp then suddenly stopped. "Are you okay?"

"Yes. And no. I feel good because it was coming out anyway but it's still upsetting. And real. And infuriating that I have to go through this shit." My tears burned hot. "And I'm sad and scared and I'll be bald for the next six months and that's fucked! Apart from that, I'm completely fine, thanks."

He put down the clippers, held me tightly and I sobbed into his shoulder until I had nothing left. With no words spoken for several minutes, we eventually separated and I steeled myself once more in the chair.

"At least you know your hair *will* grow back," Olaf said, trying to somehow lighten the moment, "and another upside is, you've got a good-shaped head."

"Sorry?" I dried my eyes with the back of my hand.

"You've got a good-shaped head. It's perfect."

"Really? What an odd thing to say."

"Well, it's true. I'm up close and personal and your head is a good shape."

I was bald. I was going to be bald for a little while and had to decide how to manage it. Would I wear a wig or cover up with scarves or caps or just be done with it and bare it all? In the weeks before I started losing my hair, I visited a wig shop to see what they offered. I'd never been into one before and didn't know what to expect. It was a very bad idea, traumatic in fact. I tried on one tight-fitting wig, carefully selected by the attendant but recoiled at my reflection in the mirror, burst into tears and ran from the shop gasping for air. It felt like the wind had not only been knocked out of my sails but from my lungs as well and this gut reaction meant one thing – I would *not* be wearing a wig.

I bought several plain-coloured caps and a few pretty scarves and friends had generously crocheted beanies but, after several wearings, nothing felt comfortable and nothing looked right either. After weeks of feeling awkward, of tears and frustration at not knowing what to do, I realised I needed to own my baldness and expose it to the world. I'd bare my head, along with baring my vulnerability. The decision was made and it was an empowering relief.

Over the ensuing summer months, I wore a sunhat when out and, as the days turned cooler, a favourite sage-coloured beanie helped with warmth. But mostly my head was unadorned and my baldness there for all to see. I went about trying to live a 'normal' life as best I could and mostly forgot about my naked cranium. But just because I was comfortable with it, didn't mean everyone else was and it became obvious some people were discomforted by my head's nude presence. In cafés, waiters would avoid eye contact at all costs, scurry off as quickly as they could, rue having to return with my order, then rapidly deliver it before dashing off again. In supermarkets, eye contact was avoided and some shoppers even changed aisles to avoid being near me. Once I had to stop myself from shouting, "I'm not contagious." And in a pharmacy, I overheard a woman whisper, "Should she even be out?" I desperately wanted to respond, "I AM allowed out – I made parole!"

But not all comments were hurtful. At a rare dinner out, Olaf and I were approached by a man in his mid-60s with a big grin on his face.

"Good on you, love," he said, placing his hand gently on my shoulder. "For what it's worth, I reckon you look really sexy." He tapped my shoulder and walked away looking chuffed before I could respond. I didn't know what to say anyway. I guess no reply was best.

But the reaction I heard dozens of times was, "Well, you're lucky you've got a good-shaped head."

I found it strange when Olaf had said it and it continued to feel strange every time. It got to a stage where, after a greeting and I could see someone's mouth opening, I'd make the comment with them and we'd say it in unison. They often looked bemused and shocked as a result. My only explanation is it's an instinctive and compassionate reaction to the uncomfortable thought, "What on earth am I going to say to this woman who clearly has cancer?"

I would've been happy talking about the weather or politics!

More than anything I was desperate for life to be normal, in the face of it being ridiculously abnormal and knew that continuing to work as a political media monitor, if I could, was a key plank to successfully crossing this dark treatment chasm. It'd be a mental stimulant, provide structure and routine to keep my chemo-brain active and I'd enjoy laughter and conversations with workmates for emotional buoyancy. So, I negotiated a four-day week, taking Mondays off to recover from Friday's late afternoon treatment. I was determined there be minimal disruption and impact on my colleagues. They were fully supportive through their willingness to swap shifts or cover an hour here or there and I didn't want to burden them with picking up extra work.

But as the weeks of treatment continued, the slog started taking its toll. Not so much physically, although clearly that was happening, but I started to struggle emotionally with the never-ending grind of chemo, the constant side effects and the overarching sadness at having cancer. I was sick of feeling miserable but had little energy to pull myself out of self-pity. So, I was beyond grateful that work could provide me with distraction, support, social engagement and some normality amid it all. But the one thing I knew I had to stay strong for, the one distant shining light at the end of this tunnel, was the goal we'd thankfully set several months ago – to walk the Cleveland Way.

If I had any hope of reaching that goal, I had to increase my fitness regime and build up strength and stamina. Initially, I forced myself to do 15 minutes of exercise-bike each day, even when it was the last thing I wanted to do. I occasionally managed a very slow climb of the city library's six flights of stairs in my lunch break, somehow wobbled down with trembling lactic legs, then shuffled back to work to recuperate for the rest of the afternoon. But that was only possible on the good days, the days I wasn't cribbing a half-hour sleep in the wellness room during my break or resting in a quiet space recovering from the toll of the morning, the days when nausea wasn't unbearable, the days my legs actually moved. But as treatment progressed and the cumulative side effects worsened, those days became less and less. The better days were often Thursdays, as symptoms slightly improved, but cruelly that meant the next dose was only one day away. I did what I could to reduce side effects and try to boost my mood and, once chemo was done and my body was healing, I'd crank up training and hope it was enough.

Then finally, after 162 days, it was my last day of treatment. I was a mixture of elation, relief and teetering on the verge of tears. When Olaf and I arrived for that final Friday session, my normally clear gunmetal blue eyes were cloudy and puffy and ready to spill over, but we kicked into our automatic routine and, within half an hour, the toxic liquid was in my veins doing its thing. Once I was unhooked and free to go, forever, it was my turn to ring the 'I've conquered this moment' bell.

I'd imagined the moment many times, having seen and heard others enjoy their raucous time and couldn't wait for my turn to be all smiles and cheer. But instead, I was a spluttering mess, could barely hit the bell hard enough to register a sound, my arms and my legs were weak and I could only manage a nod to caring staff as they offered their good wishes. It was intense, it was such a relief and the reality that some don't get to ring that bell, flooded me with gratitude. Olaf's face showed both pride and relief and he pulled me close into a side hug as we headed into our new world. But just as we neared the door, a voice yelled after us, "I hope I never see you again."

It was that same cheeky nurse, and I had to agree, I didn't want to see him again, either.

Day 2
SUTTON BANK TO OSMOTHERLEY
18.5 kilometres

Daylight appeared way too soon and, feeling the effects of the previous day's walk, I drifted in and out of sleep before dragging myself to the shower. As I exited the en-suite, Olaf woke making a beeline for his favourite shirt.

"I'm going to wear this again today," he beamed.

"I gathered that. I'm glad you washed it," I said holding my nose.

"I'm glad it dried! I think I'll wear it every day."

"Good idea. Hey, how's your knee feeling?"

"Don't worry about me, I'm fine. But let's just say I'll be glad to say goodbye to this goddamn thing."

Olaf's right knee, to put it bluntly, was stuffed. To be more specific, it needed to be replaced. He'd had it reconstructed in his early 20s thanks to an AFL injury, had numerous arthroscopes, cartilage snips and a few general 'clean-outs', so it was no surprise that he walked with a slight limp, which became more pronounced as he tired. What *was* a surprise was he couldn't fully straighten his leg and his knee remained slightly bent no matter what. He rarely complained about it but occasionally, as he repeatedly rubbed it, trying to get some relief, he might mention the constant, niggling ache but he always knew it would have to be replaced at some stage. That stage was booked two weeks after we'd return home from, hopefully, finishing the Cleveland Way.

"I'm going to get every last bit out of this knee," Olaf said on the bus to Helmsley. "175ks is about all it's got left, so it'll be the perfect send-off."

"But won't you be in pain the whole way?" I asked. "Surely, it's got to hurt like mad."

"Nah. I'm used to it. I'll be fine. It's *you* we need to focus on."

"Have a look at us. What a pair we are."

"What do you mean? We'll just do what we always do – walk at our own steady pace and get there in the end."

"Well, that's all there is to it then. But I am worried about us. If I don't finish the walk, it'll feel like I've failed."

"You're a duffer. Just think about things for a sec and look at what you've come through. No failure there. And everything we do on the walk is a bonus."

"I've just been looking forward to it so much. Anyway, enough about me. We've got to send your knee off with a bang."

"Hopefully not an actual bang, but yes, let's send it off in style."

With our luggage ready for collection and Olaf's backpack packed with snacks and water bottles, there was just enough room on top for some delights from Thomas the Baker. I was perhaps more excited than I should be about our day's food supply, but we wouldn't be back in Helmsley again, so had to make the most of our purchases from the bakery.

We enjoyed a buffet breakfast downstairs but today, there was no interaction with fellow walkers and so, no advice about the day's walk ahead. We knew it was 18.5 kilometres and the guidebook promised more panoramic views, but I'd hoped for some helpful insights from someone who'd walked it before because yesterday's tips and encouragement had been very useful.

Olaf enjoyed a second coffee as I crossed the market square and again inhaled the enticing smells. Even though I'd just eaten, I wanted to devour everything the bakery had to offer but somehow, managed restraint in my selection of two bulbous sausage rolls, which weren't natural companions to cheese, two pastries and a couple of apples.

When I got back, Olaf was waiting outside, our packs and poles leaning against the hotel's stone exterior. I carefully tucked the newly purchased delights away just as the taxi arrived to ferry us back to the previous day's finishing point – the Sutton Bank National Park Visitor's Centre.

It was overcast, fine and cool; in short, perfect walking weather but I'd still need a sunhat to protect my vulnerable scalp even though my hair growth was coming along. After the short ride we were at our day's starting point, backpacks were shimmied into place, shoulder straps moved as mine needed extra adjusting around my inserted breast, walking poles were poised and we set off in a westerly direction along the path towards Sneck Yate, surrounded by yellow and white wildflowers swaying in the slight breeze.

My shoulder strap needed extra adjusting as my usually untroubling breast form was bothering me. No matter how much I jiggled it, shook my bra, flicked its straps, it niggled and rubbed and continued to bite into my underarm. It was highly irritating and we'd only just started the day's walk but I'd just have to get over it and put it out of my mind. In the grand scheme of things, it was the least of my worries.

Not far along the path, we reached a small, elevated lookout with a view of the same rural plains we'd seen the day before but we were now heading east. Along the escarpment, we teetered with views over the spring-fed Gormire Lake and the bucolic panorama lifted my spirits. It reminded me just how inspiring nature can be and how it can even make you forget a bothersome bra.

"Do you reckon that's the Pennines all the way over there?" I asked.

"Maybe. They're large, whatever they are," Olaf replied. "I'm gobsmacked by that view. We're *so* lucky."

"You can say that again." I'd been about to say the same thing.

"Okay, we're *so* lucky."

"You are a goose." We chuckled.

The path was clear, although narrow and we resumed the natural rhythm we'd discovered worked for us – Olaf's blue shirt guided the way and I was happy in his wake. We took a sharp right turn, obeying the acorn-adorned way-marker which indicated it was both a Public Pathway and Bridleway and, when four approaching horses forced us into the long grass and wild orchids, it was obvious who had right of way. We'd now seen almost as many horses as we'd seen people on the Cleveland Way and I was happy for that ratio to continue.

Safely back on the path, there was a pine woodland to the left and grassland interspersed with wild red poppies to our right, an ancient stone remnant and medieval way-marker also thrown into the mix. Only five kilometres in and I was already needing to find a second (and probably third) wind. High Paradise Farm was another one and a half kilometres away and looked the ideal place for a break. So, with that destination in mind, I somehow managed to put some vim in my step.

Downhill to Boltby Forest, a sloping path took us beneath the dark, pine-scented canopy and steered us towards the light. When we emerged, it was liberating, given the thickly fragrant confinement and we had our first glimpse of the moorland and a distant view of the terrain we would soon encounter.

Another kilometre along, a sign pointed to our intended sit-down spot, which was now only a few hundred metres away.

It felt like tough going so far this morning, despite the beauty around us and I knew it shouldn't have taken this much out of me given it was a relatively easy section. My toe had that slight burn again and my bra was driving me mad and I couldn't work out why.

"I need to stop here for a bit," I said, heading for a garden table located away from the tea rooms. "I'm struggling this morning and I'm pretty sure a sausage roll would help." I wasn't actually sure but it was worth a try.

"Okay. Has to be a short break though, we've still got a long way to go," Olaf said, dodging chooks dancing at his feet.

"I know. There's no need to remind me. I just need this now, then I'll be fine. I hope they don't mind us sitting here." Again, it felt as though we were trespassing.

"I'm sure they don't mind. Their chickens are certainly happy to see us."

They'd busied themselves around my feet too and were clearly right at home fossicking for flecks of our pastry crumbs. We'd save the cheese for a longer break later on.

After 15 short minutes, the break was over and I felt physically and emotionally refreshed and ready to tackle the remaining 13 kilometres. A quick tidy up, big glugs of water, a reposition of packs and we were on our way.

"Excuse me," a man said as he approached, his dog already racing up the road, "do you know how far it is to Osmotherley?" He slowed down but the dog continued.

"Not exactly sure," said Olaf, "about 13 kilometres, I think. That's where we're heading."

"Oh, right you are. Lovely day for it."

"It is. And where have you walked from?" Olaf asked.

"I parked my car at Sutton Bank and thought Osmotherley and back might be a good walk."

"Wow!" I blurted. "Gee. That's a long way. You certainly put our dog walks to shame."

"Where have you walked from, then?" he asked, craning his head looking for his dog.

"Sutton Bank too," Olaf said, "but we're only going one way."

The man continued walking up the path. "Enjoy the walk."

"That's a decent walk," I said. "I've absolutely got to toughen up."

My leg muscles took a few minutes to warm up and get into the swing of it again as we walked the Hambleton drove road, an ancient drovers' path once used to move Scottish cattle to English markets. It was humbling to walk this historic road and realise centuries before, it was nothing like the curated and cared-for trail it was today. How did shepherds manage on their less-than-comfortable treks? They certainly didn't have the purpose-built walking shoes we have, but their shepherds' poles would've probably given our sticks a run for their money.

Almost two kilometres on, we returned to oppressive forest for several hundred metres, then emerged on a rutted road reaching Steeple Cross, a standing stone, and a long, dry-stone wall extending as far as the eye could see. It went on and on towards the horizon.

We walked beside this infinite boundary wall with unchanging scenery and I was glad we'd chosen not to tackle Hadrian's Wall Walk, although I was beginning to think maybe the walks had chosen me, not the other way around. The ongoing visual monotony made it feel like we weren't making any progress, with no encouraging way-markers or landmarks to get our bearings.

I was excited to see an object, something different, 100 metres ahead but couldn't quite make it out – even if I squinted. As I got closer, I could see there were remnants of an attempted wall repair which had long been abandoned, with a few tools scattered around and simply left to rust.

"Looks like an ancient smoko site," I said to Olaf walking ahead.

"Have a look at this," he laughed, now several metres in front. "If that's not some sort of sign, I don't know what is."

"OH-MY-GOD! I don't believe it. That's ridiculous."

"Hop in." He bent down and righted the rusted-out wheelbarrow.

"I actually can't believe it. That is *definitely* a sign but is it a good sign or a bad sign?"

"Not sure. But it's not quite up to the task anyway, so I'm afraid you're just going to have to walk the rest of the way."

"Right. In that case, so will you!"

"Last chance to hop in." He wobbled it towards me.

"Stop it, you goose."

"Okay. Looks like smoko is over then. Better crack on, as they say."

He put the wheelbarrow back exactly as he'd found it and I gave him a big, tight hug feeling safe, supported, loved and lucky.

Lucky, loved and supported and not just by Olaf. I am blessed to have a loving family, loyal friends, helpful neighbours and accommodating colleagues, but it was the avalanche of messages of love and concern I received, when my diagnosis became known, which knocked me off my axis. Phone calls, emails, text messages, social media posts, vouchers, flowers, plants, books – so much and from expected and unexpected people. My head at the time was swirling with medical jargon – PET scans, sentinel biopsy, survival rates (hang on, I hadn't even considered I wouldn't survive), cannulas, ports – and with my emotions balancing on the edge, every heartfelt message produced at least 100 tears. I became drained and exhausted from the tsunami of goodwill. It seemed counterintuitive, but the more love and support I got, the sadder I became and the more I wanted to be left alone. I felt heartless and ungrateful but the volume of concern on some subconscious level simply reflected the severity of my diagnosis.

I lost count of the good-hearted offers to 'speak to someone who'd been through it' or hear stories of relatives who had survived and thrived. One distant friend contacted me every day for three weeks, either through text or with a phone call, practically begging me to speak to her life-long friend who had just been through 'exactly the same thing'. She insisted we were so alike it was as though we were twins and would hit it off instantly. I appreciated her concern but needed space to make sense of my upturned world, so stopped taking her calls and then didn't reply to messages. It was too much, too soon and I simply wasn't ready.

I wanted to be left alone, to work my way through the unknown quagmire ahead and would call for support *if* I needed it. I retreated into a primal mindset, wanting solely Olaf, my parents and siblings around, those people who needed no explanations, didn't need to talk at all if I wasn't up to it. Their presence, to just sit with me or chat or help find that pesky missing jigsaw piece, was enough. It was unconditional support and all I needed. The mountain of good wishes was squirreled away to reflect on another day.

We cracked on along a wide rocky path alongside the wall for another three kilometres and it seemed it was never going to end. Our initial marvelling at the structure's engineering had waned and I wanted a change of scenery to maintain my interest but we kept trudging along until we eventually reached a signposted turnoff. Hallelujah! Before we veered left, I looked back at the distance we'd covered, back all the way along the wall and felt a burst of pride and almost symbolically, the sun cut through the clouds as my mood brightened.

Having not seen another soul for miles, it came as a shock to see the man and his dog from earlier heading very quickly towards us.

"Don't tell me you're on your way back to Sutton Bank already," I said.

"No, no, I took a bit of a detour to see what's over that hill," he said.

"And?" Olaf asked.

"Turns out, a whole lot more moorland." He whistled to his dog. "Better crack on then." And he continued rapidly along the path.

"I suspect we *will* see you on your way back," I said, raising my voice as he got further away. There was another shrill whistle and the dog sprinted to his side before running ahead full of curiosity and adventure.

Grateful to hear a different voice and for the change of scenery at the Whitestone turnoff, we continued around Black Hambleton for roughly three kilometres, now flanked by pine trees, and resumed our rhythm on the descent to Square Corner. The paved path, through bracken and ready-to-bloom heather, veered down to the left where a way-marker signalled three and a half kilometres to Osmotherley. Thank you, acorn!

It wasn't just my left big toe hurting now and that pesky right bra strap still driving me crazy, I could feel my legs didn't have much left and was glad we were on the home stretch but, despite being close, I suggested another short break. Olaf wanted to push on but begrudgingly relented and we created a makeshift picnic spot amongst the thick verge foliage. I unpacked the cheese which, despite having sweat a little throughout the day, was more than ready to eat, along with the quince paste and some crackers. We shared an apple and our picnic was complete.

It wasn't a leisurely stop, only about 15 minutes and, before our muscles completely cooled, we were back on the descending path which proved more challenging than it appeared. The further we went, the more vindicated I felt for insisting on the restorative break, otherwise I was pretty sure I would've really struggled. The large paver-like stones were slippery, so progress was slow and deliberate to properly negotiate each one as the sun became veiled behind darkening, non-threatening clouds. The gradient increased for a while before we passed a small reservoir, then crossed a bridge and it felt like we'd walked a very long way since that last sign. If it was only three and a half kilometres, why weren't we there yet?

"Why even bother saying three and a half kilometres, when clearly it's not?" I said to no-one in particular just as I spotted another sign: *Osmotherley – 1.6 kilometres.*

"Yeah, right," I muttered to myself.

I dragged my feet down through woodland, over a footbridge and walked across overgrown farmland where two deer fawns frolicked. The sun's warmth had waned and evening was making its presence felt. I was adamant we'd walked at least a kilometre and a half and was on the brink of another pointless complaint but was short of energy, short of breath and short of an agreeable audience. Anyway, the final climb up steep steps called on all my sore and sapped muscles and my breathlessness ensured there was no possible chance to speak. At the top of the incline, we reached Back Lane, a private garden we had permission to access, before squeezing through a passageway then emerging into Osmotherley's bustling main square.

It was overflowing with people, which was a stark contrast to our past two days. *Where had they all been?* I wondered. It had certainly been nowhere near us. They all sat outside one or other of the two nearby pubs, relaxing and chatting loudly. Our dog-walking mate was enjoying a beer, his loyal friend at his feet and he raised his near empty glass in our direction. We waved back in acknowledgement as he downed his last mouthful, gathered his pack and gnarled walking stick, picked up his dog's lead (which wasn't attached to the hound) and disappeared through the passageway. He was about to return to Sutton Bank, all the way back along the same path. The thought of walking beside that interminable wall again made me shudder. It would be late when he got back to his car, by which time I intended to be showered, fed and relaxed.

We were staying at The Golden Lion pub which looked like another great place and was only a few, now-stiffening, steps away. We checked in and I was so eager to shower I took off my walking gear almost before Olaf had shut the room door. A quick check showed my feet were a bit worse for wear as more red rubbed spots had appeared and my left big toe needed some closer attention but I'd deal with them later. Perhaps I was in denial about what that could mean, but my overriding desire for a shower took total priority.

As I finished undressing, a large potato crisp dislodged itself and flung from my bra. I couldn't work out how on earth it got there and equally, how it was still in one piece. Surely it should've been crushed to smithereens. But there it was, one of Olaf's 'gotta have' crisps, intact and sharp-edged, having hitched a ride inside my pocketed bra. I could only assume it'd fallen down my top the night before and shimmied its way into a safe place, then poked out just enough to cause a scratchy, awkward jab near my armpit all day. How bizarre. But at least that was resolved in the best possible way. No need to worry it could be anything more serious.

The shower was hot, powerful and released its magical qualities, washing away the day's grime and weariness and any lingering crumbs. Olaf hand-washed his beloved shirt, hung it strategically to maximise drying and then revelled in the shower's voluminous water flow from the oversized showerhead. Clean and rejuvenated, we headed for the beer garden for a thirst-quenching beverage and, on the way, Olaf stashed our cheese haul in the kitchen fridge. Like Helmsley, Osmotherley is a hub for several walks, including the Cleveland Way and the famous Coast to Coast, which explained why there were so many people sitting around sharing stories and a pint. It meant there was an energetic buzz from invigorated walkers who had all done 'their' day's walk.

Across the square, a local fish and chip shop claimed to

offer the 'best in Northern England' so Olaf felt inclined to give it a go. Seafood is not high on my go-to foods but I would give it a go along with some chips. Olaf bought two fillets of fish, loads of salty chips and plenty of scratchings - the crispy bits of batter that fall into the deep fryer so popular with locals they order bags of them on their own – and we tucked into the lot.

With our bellies full of a British culinary classic, which was enjoyable but hoped we might find better, we ordered another drink and relaxed in the cool evening ambience. My muscles reminded me we'd done back-to-back walking days, albeit on relatively moderate tracks, but we'd covered 35 kilometres and so far, it was going to plan.

I was about to call it a night, when a small group of day-walkers at an adjacent table started to chat - one of the great things about walkers – about their day. The group of four had done a lengthy loop walk and had previously finished the Coast to Coast. They'd also walked the Cleveland Way and I was eager for any snippets of advice.

"I've read that day three can be the trickiest, is that right?" I asked the group, hoping I'd misread that bit.

"It's arduous," a gnarly, fit-looking man said, "and unrelenting."

"Oh, that's the wrong answer. Now I'm *really* worried."

It was not what I wanted to hear. If *he* found it difficult, how on earth was I going to manage? No amount of cheese was going to get me through an 'arduous and unrelenting' day. Then, maybe he reacted to the horror on my face or perhaps registered my wispy, post-chemo hair, but he was keen to tell me more.

"If you're interested, there *is* a path that skirts around two of the harder climbs." My ears pricked up, I nodded and smiled. "Frankly, if I did it again, I'd take that path every time. It saves you all the heartache and you don't miss much scenery. I'd say do that but, you know, obviously it's up to you."

I wanted to jump up and kiss him, so it was probably a

good thing every muscle in my body blanketed that possibility. We listened intently to all he had to offer before a natural end to the discussion ensued. I must've thanked him at least 10 times for sharing his tips. Knowing there was an alternative route for the following day, the day I'd had the most concerns about, was a game-changer. I'd clearly developed a lot of subconscious angst about it and now felt like a worry had been lifted. I still had concerns about my stamina and my feet but I was now also concerned that if we didn't take the official route, did it mean we'd somehow cheated? But then again, who would we be cheating? It was our journey to take and if we were okay with taking a shortcut, then that was okay. We'd see how we felt when we got there.

The square slowly thinned out as walkers resumed their lives and the evening properly set in. We returned to our spacious upstairs room and Olaf's grin told me everything.

"I'm wearing this again tomorrow," he announced, checking to make sure his shirt was dry.

"Oh, no shit, Sherlock."

"There's no need to be like that."

"Sorry. No shit, Hercule. Is that better?"

"Not really. What are you going to wear? That's the big decision of the day."

"No, it's not. The big decision is which cheese to have."

"Seriously. You and your cheese obsession."

"Well, we've got to eat it. So, what do you think if we finish the Coolea and I'll grab some other goodies in the morning."

"Sounds good. But don't forget there's that café along the way that chap told us about. Lord Stones, was it?"

"Something like that. He mentioned a lot of stones but I think that was it. I'm sure we'll find it, whatever it's called."

"I'm done. Time for sleep." He was somehow already in bed. "Sweet ones."

I was about to check on Olaf's knee, but he'd already closed his eyes and I didn't want to disturb him now. I was exhausted too but dilly-dallied about until the time had come to look at my feet. It was soon obvious my left big toe was developing a very large blister. Two smaller blisters had arrived without notice on the back of my right heel and I'd ignored the sting of plantar fasciitis, a piercing inflammatory condition felt under the heel, in the same foot.

My toenails were passable, although their chalkiness offered little protection to the toes beneath and the skin surrounding the nailbed was red and flaky. All in addition to the already bulging bunions flaring red beneath protective plaster. Some serious attention would be needed in the morning, to make sure everything made it through another day.

Day 3
OSMOTHERLEY TO CLAY BANK
17.5 kilometres

I woke up nervous about the big day ahead. Even the guidebook warned it was strenuous, so I knew we had our work cut out and, despite the intel we'd received about the alternative path, I would try not to take any shortcuts or cut corners where possible. This was Olaf's walk too and it probably wouldn't be fair on him.

I got up and started the pre-breakfast routine with a focus on the day's snacks. The cheese was still in good condition, as the cheesemonger had advised and, as I put it in Olaf's pack, I gave silent thanks that he carried the weighty cargo.

Olaf woke soon after and we went downstairs for a fortifying breakfast. I felt we needed extra energy today and so I tucked into a full cooked offering, rather than the lighter options of the days before. I knew walkers who obsessed about food, making sure they were well-fed and well-stocked and now, here I was fitting that mould. Food, food, food - I was just like them – always wondering what I'd have for breakfast or whether we had enough snacks, where the nearest tea rooms were on the route and what I might buy from the bakery. It wasn't just a celebration of not feeling constantly nauseous, although that was cause for celebration, I love food. It gives me joy and often provides incentive as I plod along a path. If there's an ice-cream to be found in the next village, watch me pick up my pace. If there's Devonshire tea on offer somewhere, I'll practically run to their door.

"Hello? Hello?" Olaf waved his hand in front of my face. "Do you want another coffee or are you keen to get going?"

"Um. I think I'll grab another one this morning." I figured more caffeine had to be a good thing. "But we still should make an early start, for sure."

As I drained the second cup, I watched our bags being expertly loaded into the back of the Sherpa van, the luggage transport service we'd hired, stacked like a Mondrian artwork around the bags already on board. Our belongings would be delivered to the Buck Inn, our accommodation for the night, leaving us with just the day's necessities to lug around on our backs.

We hit the path and it was an immediate wake-up call to my legs as the initial innocuous-looking slope proved much harder than it appeared. Half a block up the hill was the village store and I headed in for bananas, a bread stick, tomato and some chocolate. They'd be perfect accompaniments to today's cheese supply, which was not just the body's fuel but also the 'carrot' dangled in front of me to keep me on the move.

"I can carry these," I said, showing Olaf what I'd bought. "I know it's the heavy stuff but I'll manage."

He was already heading up the hill, so raised his walking pole in acknowledgement, then turned back towards me.

"Let me know if it gets too much," he said, "and I'll find room in mine." I wasn't sure if he was being sarcastic but I knew it was true.

We got into a solid rhythm and were making good pace, but after half an hour of motoring along, the instructions didn't add up. No landmarks matched and we hadn't seen one way-marker anywhere along the track. Of all the days for this to happen, this would be the worst and we had no idea where we must've gone wrong. We umm-ed and ahh-ed about whether to keep going and maybe find a sign or whether to admit defeat, retrace our steps and work out where we were. We were tersely exchanging our thoughts when a council van approached and I breathed a sigh of relief. Of all the possible people to come past at that moment, a council worker was ideal.

"Hello, mate," Olaf said, "we think we might've missed a turn off for the Cleveland Way walking trail. Don't suppose you know if we're on the right track, by chance?"

"Um. Oh, let's see. What was that name again?" the driver asked.

"The Cleveland Way," we both replied.

"The Cleveland Way, you say. Nah, no, sorry. Never heard of it." He shook his head. "Turrah." Then drove off.

We were now 45 minutes into the walking day and barely taken a step on the designated path. I swore loudly and also under my breath as we backtracked towards Osmotherley. All the while, Olaf ignored me. We arrived back at the outskirts of the village after 30 minutes of my cursing, where as clear as anything there was a way-marker pointing to the right.

"How on earth did we miss that?" I asked, then realised it was where I'd been a smart-arse offering to carry the heavy load, which must've distracted us.

"No idea," Olaf replied. "Couldn't be any clearer. Still, we're here now so let's get started."

With well over an hour wasted and valuable energy used, the possibility of a three-kilometre side trip to Mount Grace Priory was off the table and we left the village under a grey, overcast sky. It perfectly mirrored my now gloomy mood, but I had to snap out of the crankiness and try and enjoy the beautiful surrounds. I dived into my pocket in search of my lip balm, as a fresh application always picks me up, and found something jammed into the bottom corner. It felt like a nut, its familiar shape emerging as I rolled it in my fingertips. It turned out to be a smooth, beret-capped acorn. I had no idea how it got there but discovering it right then was perfect. This symbol of the trail, along with potential and positivity, had been found right when I needed it and made me smile. I took some slow, deep breaths as I clasped it and my self-indulgent funk dissipated before I fell calmly into step behind Olaf, who was already soldiering ahead.

I'd clearly been distracted and hadn't noticed the kissing gate ahead as Olaf had already manoeuvred through it and, as was our new tradition, stood expectantly across the railings before I knew what was happening. I obliged with a kiss and was instantly allowed through. I loved how the kissing gates added some unexpected joy and brightened up the day as we walked along. Even the weather now followed suit, having shaken off its moodiness, with gentle sunshine adding some extra pep to our pace. It felt like we were traversing hillsides and woodlands in good time, even with the earlier hiccup, and needed for that to continue across the day's remaining kilometres. And then my left toe started to hurt as I'd stupidly only given it minor attention earlier and feared I might pay a price for such neglect. I'd have to check it later – properly this time.

The terrain then flattened out as we passed an out-of-place transmitter station and Olaf, once again, marvelled at the drystone walls crisscrossing the land. Over a hill, the path descended through an ordinary gate and the vista opened out. A National Trust sign for Scarth Wood Moor greeted us as the path ahead stretched kilometres into the distance. I stopped to take in what we faced over the next few days until I noticed something on the horizon.

"Oh, my goodness! See that tiny pyramid-shaped thing over there?" I asked, pointing slightly to the left into the distance. "That's Roseberry Topping, where we're supposed to be staying tomorrow night." We stood in silence as the monumental task sunk in.

"Right. God, it's incredible how much ground we'll cover in a couple of days," Olaf said. "So long as we keep moving. But how are you feeling?"

"More tired than I'd hoped. I probably need to take a break fairly soon."

"Good idea. Let's get to that next rise and find a suitable spot. My knee could do with a rest too."

It was unlike Olaf to mention his knee, so it must've been sore. Or was it that trick your mind plays on you when you near the end of something that it suddenly becomes your only focus? Either way, I had to remember he was overcoming physical hardship too, even though he never complained or grizzled (unlike me) and needed some support.

So, with a nod, we headed east along the long, clear path towards our very distant, clearly visible target. We entered a woodland along a forestry path and continued placing one foot in front of the other for about a kilometre and then, I really needed a break. Surely that rise we were aiming for was getting close now. No, apparently not, and we kept going through grassland, tiptoed over fords and every part of me ached. My feet were burning, my mind wouldn't focus and I desperately needed to stop, but a steep climb had other ideas as Olaf powered ahead. I managed 20 steps then stopped to catch my breath, then another 20 steps and another breath-catching stop. I was crawling up at a snail's pace but there was no other way to do it. Olaf eventually stopped and waited until I caught up.

"This isn't even the hard bit of the day," I managed between gasps. "I'm already buggered and this is apparently the easy bit."

"Look, we're in no hurry," he said. "We'll just take our time and we'll get there, like we always do. You know we will."

I burst into tears. "I need a rest. And some food. And a hug."

He wrapped his arms around me and pulled me into his chest and, despite the sweat, it was the only place I wanted to be. He could always defuse my hotheadedness, give selfless and unwavering support and he'd done it once again, just with a hug. We disentangled, I blew my nose, took a few deep breaths and was ready to continue to our resting spot. Thankfully, the gradient then plateaued on Live Moor, and the view behind us showed exactly where we'd come from. After roughly nine kilometres, the halfway point of the day's walk, it was time to stop for lunch – finally.

I sat on a suitably flat rock, guzzled some water, busied myself unpacking the goodies from the pack next to me and delighted in the relief at taking the weight off my feet.

"G'day there, fellas," Olaf said with extra Aussie twang.

I quickly looked around, expecting to see some walkers behind us but instead, it was a herd of curious, shaggy-coated, black-faced sheep, looking at us from a respectful distance. If I'd given it proper thought, we'd scarcely seen another person all day; in fact, it felt like we could've been the only humans at all on the moors. Little wonder the sheep were taken aback at us being there.

It felt so good to stop and rest. My legs hummed and I didn't let myself think about what might be happening to my feet, so I focused on stuffing the bread stick with tomato and crumbly cheese and handed the delicious makeshift sandwich to Olaf. He quickly bit into it and a tomato seed squirted onto his much-loved shirt. I went to pick it off but figured he'd be washing it later anyway.

"Is it Friday today? I think it's Friday, isn't it?" I asked, having lost track of overall time, while focusing on smaller moments during our walk.

"Yep. Today's Friday alright."

"Just think what we were doing this time on Friday seven weeks ago. I know which one I'd rather be doing."

"Oh, for sure. God, it's been seven weeks already. Mind you, some things haven't changed."

"I think it's funny how throughout this whole thing: the surgery, chemo, the works, all I wanted was for everything to just be normal. I busted my gut to keep life, everything, as normal as I could. And now, it's all over and everything *is* normal I feel like I shouldn't be living a normal life. Does that make sense? I feel like, unless I *do* something with my life then it's wasted. I should have an epiphany or take a new direction or free myself from the limits I put on myself and just take on the world. But I'm back living a normal life, exactly as I wanted it to be and, somehow, it now feels abnormal."

"I think I get it, sort of. But you *are* doing something out of the ordinary right here, right now, particularly given you're still healing. Isn't that enough?"

"I suppose so. No, you're right, of course, it's amazing given what my body has been through. I don't know. It's really hard to express and probably even harder to understand, I don't completely understand it myself. But the one thing I was so desperate for – normality – doesn't sit comfortably right now. Like you said, things haven't changed and yet they have."

"Well, all I was thinking was it's Friday afternoon and we're eating cheese again. That's all. Sorry for being glib."

"It's just I haven't been able to verbalise this until now. And, you know, perhaps my epiphany is yet to come. I hope so. Is there a time limit on epiphanies?"

"Not as far as I know but I'm no epiphany expert. What I *do* know is you'll find your 'thing' at some stage, just allow yourself time."

"Mmmmmm. I just don't want to have gone through all this for nothing."

"For nothing? For nothing? You might want to think about that."

We ate under the gaze of our fleecy companions, along

with their occasional bleat, soaking in the soul-enriching effects of nature. The sun, fresh air and lush patchwork of fields were a salve for my rejuvenating body, even though my legs still felt heavy and my hips held a deep ache. We were into our third day of walking and my gnawing concern about finishing was building like a tidal wave of doubt about to crash. Perhaps we should've grabbed that wheelbarrow when we had a chance yesterday.

I stood and shook out my legs to see if they still worked and the rush of blood to the muscles seemed to kick them into gear. A few more vigorous shakes and I was ready to continue, at least for a bit longer and hoped to quickly fall into the rhythmic trance that comes after some initial resistance. So, with our backpacks repacked and walking poles ready, I double-tapped Olaf on the backside as a signal to push on and we were back on our way. I glanced ahead at the path stretching before us and thought Roseberry Topping seemed a little closer or maybe that was wishful thinking.

There was no time for that as we immediately faced a steep descent on large stone steps which was a worry for Olaf's knee. Heading down steps always caused him pain and with his joint the way it was in the last few days, I knew this must feel like a skewer piercing him with each landing but he continued without a sign it may have been an issue. Getting to the bottom was slow going to make sure we didn't tumble but we made it down safely before we had to cross a main road which seemed totally out of place.

Our path passed right by the Lord Stones Café which, if you didn't know it was there, could easily be missed as it was camouflaged by a stand of large trees and built into a bank like a bunker. But we were looking out for it and stopped for a coffee, even though it hadn't been long since our last break. We sat outside in the sunshine as people at neighbouring tables tucked into nice-looking pies and, without saying a word, Olaf went inside and returned with two homemade chunky steak delights which, despite having only just eaten, we tucked away nicely. I suggested letting them settle before setting off for the toughest section of the day but it was just a convenient delaying tactic. I was definitely procrastinating and Olaf had other ideas anyway.

We refilled our water, whacked on our packs, I twice-tapped Olaf's backside and we were back on the path again. A fence guided us at first, then gradually the path became steeper until we reached Cringle Moor at 400 metres altitude. Perhaps the pie had given me a surge of energy but the climb didn't seem too taxing on my legs. Olaf suggested we sit at a seat in an ancient stone shelter but now I'd started I needed to keep moving. If I stopped now, I was sure I'd struggle to get going again. We walked along an escarpment for a small distance and then came to the inevitable descent and I braced for each jarring step as I inched my way down. I'd stopped to regather myself just as a small, wiry man ran past and, seconds later, his lean female companion zoomed by too. I think he said something about it being a lovely day but was gone in a blink and I had no time to reply as they bounded to the bottom as if on springs. I couldn't help but think how different we humans were – some bodies made for physical exertion, some less so – and at that moment I knew exactly which category I was in.

When we arrived at the bottom, a public footpath sign to Great Broughton pointed left, whereas the Cleveland Way path doglegged to the right.

"This must be the path we heard about last night," I said. "Shall we take it, or do you want to go over the top?"

"I think we take this path around the bottom," Olaf replied, glancing up at the climb to Cold Moor.

"That's the right answer. There's no way I could climb that."

"No. I don't fancy climbing it either, to be honest. And then there's the notorious Wainstones after that." We were both keen to avoid it with its steep climb followed by a scramble through, across and around this exposed rocky outcrop.

"Yep. Around the bottom it is, so long as you're okay that we're not on the official route."

"I'm completely good with it. I'd rather we take this path than not finish at all, or worse, have to carry you."

"Fair enough. And thank you. Okay, let's see where this takes us."

At first, the path was relatively easy but then turned into a thick, muddy forest which proved slippery and precarious underfoot. It was like walking on and through, thick chocolate icing which would either suck your feet down or fling you about like the final swirl at the top of the cake. Inevitably, walking was slow and deliberate to avoid tumbling over but then my right foot suddenly slid sideways and I only just managed to balance up before almost landing on my left hip, instinctively using my walking pole to stop the fall. As I slowed my breath and rubbed my twinging left knee, I flashed back to four weeks earlier when we'd visited Olaf's daughter near Byron Bay.

Chemo was three weeks behind me when we'd taken off for an overdue, mid-winter trip to visit Lucy and her partner, Dean. Free from the weekly commitment of treatment, we were happy to jump on a plane and head to the enchanting Northern Rivers in New South Wales but knew we couldn't just indulge in wholesome food and organic wine. We had to keep building my fitness even during this mini holiday. So, when Lucy suggested the Minyon Falls walk, a 13-kilometre, grade 3-rated bushwalk, with short steep hills and lots of steps, it was an ideal 'trial' for what we could expect three weeks later in Yorkshire.

We set off on the 20-minute drive inland and started the trek in the early afternoon. The tropical surroundings were large and lush and I barely noticed the steep gradient and slippery conditions. We walked along muddy paths, on much-appreciated boardwalks, scrambled over rocks and, after about an hour and a half of descending, the waterfall's thundering cascade intensified as we neared the bottom of the valley.

With only a few rocks to scramble over before reaching the base of the falls, I slipped, losing my footing and fell off a large, mossy boulder, crashing heavily straight onto my left knee. The pain was immediate and I yelled, then swore repeatedly and Olaf and Lucy, who were metres ahead, rushed back to help. I tried to right myself, like a baby giraffe taking its first steps and shooed away their offers of help, then manoeuvred myself to a suitable spot to push myself upright and did a quick body scan. All bones were intact but it was obvious my knee had suffered damage; it was already swelling before my eyes. Not great news given we were at the bottom of the valley and there was only one way out - I'd have to haul myself back up the six and a half kilometres we'd just descended.

With darkening skies and the temperature dropping, I limped and winced slowly back to the car – relieved, tired and upset. My knee was now the size of a softball and my mind raced forward to our upcoming Cleveland Way walk. Relief at having got out of the valley turned to anger at myself for adding another layer of uncertainty about our trip. On the drive home, I sobbed in silence in the backseat hoping everything would be okay if I could manage to keep myself safe in the next three weeks.

Now on the Cleveland Way, I knew another ill-timed slip or slide could easily lead to my knee flaring up. I'd have to be extra careful now on this treacherous forest floor with its booby-trapped, tricky terrain. It was dark and heavy underneath the thick canopy and my earlier relief at avoiding facing the Wainstones had started to turn to despair. I wondered if this was even the right path or whether we were too quick to deviate from the proper, marked route. After what felt like five kilometres but was likely closer to three, with a niggling knee and in the dark, muddy forest, I decided we had to be lost. Surely, by now we should've emerged from this enveloping foliage to at least see where we were headed. The thought of having to retrace our steps, then make the dreaded climb anyway was almost too much to bear. It was late afternoon and I'd started to overdramatise everything: by the time we walked back three kilometres, then over Cold Moor and somehow get past the infamous Wainstones, it would be early evening and I'd be completely shattered.

"We're lost," I said. "I knew it. We took the wrong path back there."

"It *had* to be the path," Olaf said. "Let's just keep going – it has to lead somewhere." We walked on several metres. "Hey, wait. Listen. Can you hear that?" We stopped.

"It sounds like traffic."

"Exactly! Which means -"

"There's a road nearby. Hooray!"

"Right. It's got to be fairly close, so let's keep going, get out of this wood and see where we are."

I trudged along in a silent, yet hopeful, grump for several more minutes and then we emerged exactly where we were meant to be – at the B1257 at Clay Bank. It was the spot we were being picked up to be taken to our night's accommodation, five kilometres away. A young couple and their golden Spaniel sat beside the road looking exhausted and were surprised to see us.

"Hello," I said, "I don't suppose you're waiting for a man named Gunther, are you?"

"Yes," the Dutch-accented woman answered, "we think he will be here soon."

"Oh, that's wonderful," I said, "we were supposed to call him when we got here, but maybe now we can squeeze in with you. You're staying at the Buck Inn, I assume?"

She nodded but the quick glance between them showed they weren't keen on us muscling in on their lift. I guess if we couldn't all fit, along with their dog and all our gear, they rightly had first dibs. We weren't going anywhere and would happily wait for him to come back to collect us.

"Where did the day start for you?" she asked, adeptly changing the subject.

"Osmotherley," I replied, "and I'm *very* glad to have finished. It was tough going today. What about you - where did you start?"

"Osmotherley also. Funny that you were not seen on the path."

"Yeah. Strange how it works sometimes, isn't it?" I wasn't up to confessing our detour.

Gunther's car wasn't large but, somehow, everyone and everything squashed in and, within minutes, we were all on our way, chatting, laughing and gasping as he took the tight bends. It was a stark contrast to how I'd been feeling only 15 minutes earlier.

From the outside, The Buck Inn in Chop Gate seemed a typical English inn, but inside, Gunther's German influence was everywhere. The décor, menu and range of beers reflected his Bavarian heritage, along with his need for precision as he checked us in. He gave multiple instructions, including an offer to return us in the morning to the exact spot he'd picked us up – at 8:30am sharp. No waiting. If we missed his lift, we'd have to find our own way there. His message was loud and clear and we'd heard it. What was also obvious was how comfortable Olaf felt in this environment from the minute we'd walked through the heavy, wooden doors. His parents emigrated to South Australia from post-war Hamburg and, although his mother had died in a car accident when Olaf was only six, his father continued a number of German traditions until he passed away six years ago. Walking into this setting clearly triggered some memories.

"God, this reminds me of dad," Olaf said, as we headed to our room. "It even smells like home used to smell; it's just so familiar. The music in the bar, everything. It's really got me, I gotta say."

"I thought that glint in your eye meant you felt at home."

"I do. I just wasn't expecting it to hit me so hard out of the blue. It takes me straight back to childhood and made me sentimental, I guess. Happiness and sadness all in one. Mainly happy, but I really miss dad. Perhaps I'm just exhausted from a long day."

"Yeah, maybe, but it's so beautiful your dad gave you the gift of his culture to embrace and shape who you are. No wonder you're feeling nostalgic." It was my turn to hug him for a change.

"Well, anyway, I'm definitely looking forward to embracing one of those German beers I noticed."

"You noticed the beers and I noticed the menu. Sounds about right. Now, if you're okay, I totally need a shower."

"I'm okay. Thanks. Sehr gut. Danke."

While I washed away the day's muck, Olaf washed his shirt, removing that pesky tomato seed which had stuck like glue. He then spent ages in the shower negotiating its fickle thermostat. We headed into the darkly furnished bar and collapsed into its deep club lounge seats. Getting lost in Osmotherley now seemed like forever ago, along with the full range of emotions we'd experienced in one day and, as I overheard a woman say she thought the Cleveland Way *really packed a punch*, after three days and 52 kilometres, I had to agree.

We settled in for a second pint of Erdinger Dunkel, as the young Dutch couple sat at an adjacent table. Their dog, Britt, nestled in front of an unlit fire and fell into an exhausted sleep within minutes, letting out a snore to remind us she was there. As we chatted, I was surprised and gladdened to learn they'd also found the day's walk strenuous. And when Claudine said, *particularly over the stones at the end, it was not so nice*, I gave silent thanks we'd taken the lower path, even with its own challenges.

On all the walks we've done over the years, we'd found

walkers love nothing more than to chat about their aches and pains, their different schedules and the variety of accommodation arrangements. And so, we found out the Dutch couple were tenting along the Cleveland Way to give flexibility to their planned seven-day timeframe and would be clearly covering many more kilometres than us each day. Britt let out another loud snore and we laughed at the joy of living a dog's life.

Another couple entered the bar and I instantly recognised them as the 'speedy' couple who'd bounded past us back on the path, so it was odd they'd taken this long to arrive. I was later told they'd run from the pick-up point on the B1257 to the Buck Inn – an extra five kilometres – for the fun of it. Yep, I thought again, we are all made up *very* differently.

Plates of sauerkraut, bratwurst and goulash arrived and I now wondered if the glint I'd seen earlier in Olaf's eye had actually been a small tear. I thought I glimpsed it again but whatever it was, it quickly dissipated as our well-developed appetites took hold and we tucked in. The next time I looked up, the Dutch couple and their dog had gone. They must've headed back to their tent pitched in the pub's garden and I wondered whether we'd see them again after our drop off in the morning. I supposed not, given our differing schedules but was 100% sure we wouldn't see the 'speedy' couple again unless they lapped us on their second time around.

It was only around 8:00pm but the effects of the day's exertion, including getting lost twice, kicked in and my eyes didn't want to stay open. It was time to head back to our modest room and prepare for the morning as we had to be packed and ready, finished breakfast and be at Gunther's car by 8:30am. Sharp!

Olaf checked his beloved shirt – it was dry, of course – and I started organising the packs for the morning before I knew I had to deal with my feet. I faffed about deciding on cheese and other snacks for the 15.5-kilometre walk and, as I pondered that distance, my leg muscles tightened and hips silently screamed. We still had six days and 125 kilometres to go and I didn't know how on earth I was going to do it. I wasn't sure I had the physical strength for it, but my mental strength was waning too, probably because I was tired. I'd spent seven months desperately focusing on this walk and hoped I wasn't going to crumble a third of the way in. Perhaps it had been a stupid idea all along and we should've postponed the trip all those months ago. Or perhaps, it was just a tough day and tomorrow I'd feel differently. Overwhelmed by fatigue and doubt, I decided to deal with my feet in the morning.

IMMUNITY

The sole purpose of chemotherapy is to obliterate cancer cells but there's the collateral damage of wiping out healthy cells too. It's like cracking a walnut with a sledgehammer but until targeted treatments develop further, it's the only approach we have. So, it's little wonder the immune system takes a massive hit as the bone marrow struggles to produce white blood cells, meaning defences are weakened and the body becomes vulnerable to infection. A common cold, if caught during treatment, can be more severe and prolonged and could potentially delay a chemo session until it's gone. As I was on a tight, self-imposed treatment schedule anyway and didn't want any postponement to that timetable, I had to be diligent with hygiene standards to minimise any exposure to germs. So, I was often perplexed during my Friday afternoon doses when oncology nurses, clad in their purple protective capes, would ask, 'Are you doing anything exciting on the weekend?'

I'd reply that I'd see how I felt or I'd be laying low, but apart from not feeling like doing anything even remotely considered exciting, I couldn't risk getting sick. I'd been instructed not to take Vitamin C, echinacea or zinc as I normally would, as those natural immunity-boosting supplements interfered with the chemo process. But I *was* fortunate to be given Neulasta, a bone marrow stimulating injection to be self-administered the day after treatment.

This 'super-shot', which normally cost a staggering $1,200, was included in my treatment bundle and, when Olaf arrived home from work on a Saturday afternoon, he jabbed the precious liquid into my tummy fat. He injected me four times during the first round of chemo - every three weeks for 12 weeks – and was another situation we *never* imagined we'd have to go through. When I moved to round two of 12 weekly sessions, with the drug Paclitaxel now circulating, there was no need for the expensive immunity booster and Olaf could go back to his official school job rather than 'moonlight' as a nurse. I offered to give him a glowing reference if he ever wanted or needed one.

I continued to work four days a week with the big challenge of trying to avoid contact with others as much as possible - a tricky task in a populated, 12-storey, city-based office block. I considered wearing a face mask but thought it would feel claustrophobic and draw too much attention and, as I tried to go about my days flying under the radar and behaving as usual, a mask was not an option. I was mindful to wash my hands fastidiously and regularly, tried to coordinate my use of lifts sparingly and moved to a separate office to minimise human contact. My fabulous workmates supported whatever was needed, even occasionally pulling a funny face through the glass wall to cheer me along. If I could bottle and prescribe their capacity to lift me up just at the right time, I would, with the recommended dose taken, not through a cannula or port but with one big swig straight from that bottle.

Everything somehow worked. I had no infections, no colds, no flu, no coughs and no need for an extension to my final chemo date. I succumbed to the odd mouth ulcer and noticed cuts took longer to heal, but my immunity miraculously held up and fought the good fight. Once again, those words echoed in my ears, *You might surprise yourself how well you'll come through all this.* I was definitely surprised and delighted.

I couldn't wait for my body to bounce back to health once chemo had finally finished. It even started bouncing weeks before the final treatment. Fluffy, blonde, babylike hair was my new look and I loved the Annie Lennox vibe (well, maybe I wasn't that cool but that's how I felt) and I thought I'd made a good start along the healing path. But two weeks after I'd rung that bell, thinking I was clear of all those toxins, my eyes puffed up like a goldfish and my fingernails and toenails turned dirty brown. Apparently, it is a common reaction to the body purging lingering chemicals. I was now less Annie Lennox and more Billy Idol on a really bad day but hoped to be belting out *Would I Lie to You?* again very soon.

My oversized eyes deflated a couple of days later, but the stained nails were there for the long haul, to grow out millimetre by millimetre. Otherwise, I felt physically stronger every day, looked well and my skin was a healthy pinkish hue. A visit to the dental hygienist was another checklist task to tick along my recovery road.

"Your teeth are in pretty good shape," she said. "You brush and floss regularly?"

"Well, I brush twice a day, but I probably don't floss as much as I should. I look after them as best I can but they've taken a hit during chemo."

"It's so important that you brush often," she said, paused, then added, "especially with you being a smoker."

Had I heard correctly? Had she just said I was a smoker? She had. I was too shocked at first to respond and my mouth was prised open with instruments prodding around but I felt compelled to reply when she turned to her tray.

"I don't smoke. Never have," I said.

"Okay, if you say so. But I can tell. Your fingernails don't lie."

I was stunned and felt vulnerable in a reclined position, so it took a few moments to register the comment. Instinctively, I clenched my hands and hid my nails or, perhaps my fists reflected my angry desire. Her unexpected words were like a punch to my solar plexus and I remained speechless. She kept chiselling away, unconcerned or unaware of her insensitivity and I was grateful to be wearing light-protective glasses so she couldn't see my tear-filled eyes. But, as she continued her work, I realised it didn't matter if she thought I smoked; it was irrelevant to my healing, even if that wasn't quite as advanced as I'd thought or hoped. She finished her task, raised me to a seated position; I rinsed my mouth and took a deep, composing breath deciding the truth was always best outed.

"I don't smoke, I have never smoked and I will never smoke. I have, however, just finished six months of chemotherapy and these fingernails are a result." I proudly held out my hands as a badge of honour. "So, I guess things aren't always as they might appear." I wriggled out of the chair, grabbed my bag and headed for the door, hoping maybe she might spare someone else hurtful or incorrect assumptions.

"If you say so," she said again. "See you in six months."

No, you won't. I would be looking for another hygienist.

Day 4
CLAY BANK TO KILDALE
15.5 kilometres

It was a disrupted sleep despite my exhaustion. The double bed was uncomfortable and, with every turn, I worried I'd either kick or jab Olaf or somehow interrupt his sleep. I tried to lay as still as I could for most of the night but was fully awake well before I needed to be. I was used to less than perfect sleep these days, thanks to chemotherapy and night sweats and, of course, thanks to menopause, which was now well entrenched. I'd had the odd hot flush before breast cancer showed up - being in my early 50s it was to be expected - which were annoying and always inconvenient. They'd turn my face the colour of an over-ripe tomato, accompanied by a heavy sweat across my top lip, the nape of my neck, across my forehead, everywhere. But given their relative infrequency, they were manageable, mainly thanks to a large, foldable fan which became my constant companion. It was the first thing in my handbag before I went anywhere. Other than that, early menopause wasn't too bad - my body shape stayed the same, my libido hadn't diminished, I had minor mood swings (no more than usual), a few aches and pains, but overall felt able to navigate through this phase quite well.

Fast forward to life after chemotherapy and the world of

hormonal therapy, a key plank in successfully stopping certain cancer cells from growing, and welcome to taking Tamoxifen or Letrozole (oestrogen-reducing medication) for a minimum of five to 10 years. Reading the long list of possible side effects was frightening and I was full of trepidation but not taking it was like gambling with your life, like playing Russian roulette with my DNA. Anyway, I'd coped with chemo so I was sure I could cope with this, even if it meant a rapid plunge into full menopause.

Within weeks of starting, a myriad of menopausal symptoms arrived. Intense hourly hot flushes, often lasting up to 10 minutes, were preceded by a sensation in my feet as though razor blades under my soles were trying to cut their way to freedom which, along with the neuropathy, felt like a continual onslaught. My body shape changed instantly as a spare tyre around my middle seemed to appear overnight and clothes, which had fitted only weeks before, were now tight and uncomfortable. The scales reflected a small weight gain, but the distribution of weight had definitely shifted.

My confidence and self-esteem plummeted, something I was battling anyway with my changed and scarred body, and I sunk into a trough of sadness. My skin sagged in new places and its pigmentation changed. I felt fat, ugly and disfigured, as though it was impossible to look nice, let alone attractive. I worried about how Olaf now saw me and whether his desire would disappear along with my waistline and, as my libido seeped away with the remaining traces of oestrogen, I felt very old, helpless and deflated.

I'd lie awake covered in sweat, struggling with conflicting emotions. I hated how I felt and looked but then was grateful for simply being alive with a positive prognosis. I knew in another era, not that many years ago, I wouldn't be so lucky, in fact, I'd probably be dead. So many people weren't as fortunate as me and so I'd berate myself for the indulgent self-pity occurring in the middle of the night. Until I realised all these feelings were valid, it wasn't as simple as one side overriding the other. It was okay to struggle with these big issues and feel them simultaneously or feel them at different times in different situations. But they did mainly happen, as is often the way, when I couldn't sleep in the early hours of the morning.

With a bit of time, I adjusted to, or accepted, menopausal life. The hot flushes continued to flare with less frequency and intensity, I try to manage my weight but my waistline still hasn't returned but the glint in Olaf's eye is still there, as is his knack of making me feel special.

The Buck Inn's resident rooster let out a faint, warm-up crow to announce the morning's arrival. It had been light for hours so he was late to the game but with his duty done, he could strut around confidently for the rest of the day. Olaf's soft, steady breathing assured me he hadn't heard him, so I began a mental to-do list to finish before breakfast. The number one priority was to check my feet, to see if any more blisters had popped up and a close second was to see how my nails had coped. I knew our backpacks were 90% packed, our luggage was ready for collection, except for toothbrushes, so everything there was in order, but the checklist had made me restless and it was time to get up. A loud groan involuntarily escaped as I swung my legs out of bed.

"What was that?" Olaf asked, rolling to face me.

"My body letting me know it was a big day yesterday. Gee, my hips are really sore. And so are my knees and my shoulders and God my -"

"I get the message - you're sore. Which is a good thing. It means you've actually *done* something." He managed to get out of bed without a single groan.

"Of course I've done something. We've walked more than 50 kilometres in three days, which I know hasn't broken any world records but it's solid. And my sad and sorry muscles are letting me know about it. That's all."

"I think I'll wear this shirt today."

"What a surprise! I didn't expect that." I toned it down this time.

A glance at my feet confirmed a huge, busted blister on my left big toe. The pain had been masked by nerve numbness, but I knew I'd been neglectful and now there was a real chance of infection unless I dealt with it immediately. The two smaller blisters on my right heel hadn't worsened but still needed careful treatment but the real concern was both big toenails looking like they were crumbling. I could manage the blisters, could walk through the discomfort but my toenails needed to stay solid for us to finish. I swabbed the open blister with antiseptic, then applied various band-aids to all three spots to try to absorb the friction. Bunion pads were affixed, then I wound cotton bandaging around my big toenails in an effort to hold them together. I sprinkled Blistershield powder into my socks, dusted it around for an even spread, put them aside before finishing getting dressed. I'd leave putting on my socks and shoes until the very last minute.

"Oh, my Lord, have a look at your feet," Olaf said.

"I know. You can hardly see them under all the tape. I hope it all works."

"You could always wrap them in bubble wrap if it doesn't. But I reckon you'll be okay."

"Actually, these gel plasters are a bit like that. Now, there's an idea, socks made out of bubble wrap. I reckon they'd be great!"

"I'd say there's a reason they don't already exist. Probably a few reasons, actually. Now, it's time to put on your regular bamboo socks and your shoes and let's get to breakfast."

I chose a lighter breakfast, as last night's German feast was still digesting and I couldn't face anything heavy. There was scarcely time to enjoy the fruit, yoghurt and coffee or stock up with any of the slices on offer, before Gunther was calling. We downed final mouthfuls, grabbed our gear and dashed outside towards our impatient-looking host. The Dutch couple, with Britt in tow, flung themselves into the car and we tore off to the day's starting point - Urra Moor – where we landed after about five minutes. They tumbled from the Volkswagen and the dog and her owners were up the hill and out of sight as we still gathered our belongings. Gunther stuck his head out the window.

"Enjoy some King George whiting for me please, when you get home," he said, having lived in South Australia years ago. "It's the best fish I've ever eaten. And please, have it with some riesling from the Clare."

"Alright then," Olaf said, "we'll do it just for you."

"I'm not crazy about fish but the King George we had on Kangaroo Island last year *was* delicious," I added.

"Oh, Kangaroo Island is spectacular. Honestly, I don't understand why you'd travel to the UK when you live in paradise," Gunther said. "I mean it. You live in paradise. I hope you know this."

"We do," Olaf said.

"We're very lucky," I said, "and we'll definitely say *Prost!* next time we enjoy that whiting. Thanks again for looking after us."

"My pleasure." He waved and sped off.

Immediately, we faced a steep path up towards Kildale. My stubborn muscles were reluctant to move and we started walking at a snail's pace but at least we knew we were on the right path, unlike yesterday. There was, however, confusion about our day's ultimate destination. Our accommodation was booked at the King's Head Inn at the base of Roseberry Topping, but our guidebook pointed us to Kildale, seven kilometres short of there. As huffing and puffing took over, as we climbed to the day's high point – Round Hill – I figured we'd work it out later. The gradient soon flattened, allowing me to catch my breath and a way-marker indicated Bloworth Crossing was 5.5 kilometres away.

Along dirt paths, scattered with tiny pebbles, a quick look around revealed we were now properly on top of the moors. The multihued patchwork of fields spanning the horizon were lush and vibrant, and, even under Yorkshire's slightly overcast skies, a closer carpet of heather appeared to glimmer. We'd covered roughly five kilometres and despite my body's initial resistance, I now felt stronger and warmed up. Even my feet felt okay, thanks to all the bandaging. At least, I hoped the bandaging was doing its job.

The path widened and we navigated around large puddles laying across the surface as a light breeze accompanied us across the open moorland. We'd been lucky to have missed the obvious recent rain and avoid stronger winds which would've made this stretch challenging and uncomfortable. The weather gods, who could be fickle, were smiling on us today.

For a change, we walked side by side in silence for about half a kilometre enjoying the sounds provided by Mother Nature.

"How's the serenity?" Olaf said, channelling his inner Darryl Kerrigan.

"So much serenity," I said, "we're the luckiest family in the world." I giggled, thinking how different this was to Bonnie Doon.

A nearby flock of grazing sheep looked up, surprised by our voices, but quickly returned to their tasty offerings and we returned to our easy silence. A continuous loop of *We're going to Bonnie Doon. We're going to Bonnie Doon* played in my head and I thought about *The Castle*, the Kerrigans and their unshakeable gratitude, deep love and abiding loyalty. In that sense, maybe Darryl Kerrigan and Olaf weren't too different after all.

I'd been so distracted I was surprised when our path joined a dismantled rail bed and we were already at Bloworth Crossing. The path now had two options, either continue straight or take the sharp dogleg left. The guidebook steered us left but I noticed a group of walkers a long way ahead in the distance. I checked the book again and it definitely demanded we go left as the straight path would see us joining the 307-kilometre Coast to Coast Walk. I'd leave that to the rapidly disappearing tiny specks on the horizon and was very happy to turn. We walked past ancient boundary stones, a medieval shaft and a Bronze Age burial site and the next time I looked ahead Roseberry Topping was much closer – thank goodness. The famous landmark, which had been a distant focal point, loomed closer but we still had a long way to go. We just didn't know how much longer, as we didn't really know where we were walking to.

Another kilometre on, I thought I heard faint, distant voices, but dismissed it because, apart from the odd sheep, we hadn't seen another soul all day. I reasoned it was a trick of the wind, even though that had dropped right away but then I was sure they became louder. We had a 360-degree view over the landscape and there wasn't a person to be seen. Suddenly, a small moving object came hurtling towards us. It was a charging dog hellbent on Olaf and me. We had nowhere to run or escape and our only defence would be the large rocks on the path's edge. We knew neither of us really wanted to do that, but as the dog continued to gain on us, Olaf bent down for a hefty stone which he readied in his palm.

It was so close now I could see its tongue hanging out, its ears flopping around and its tail wagging in delight.

"It's Britt!" I yelled. "Thank goodness."

"Oh, thank Christ," Olaf said. "I didn't really think it was a wild dog, but it obviously crossed my mind." He tossed the rock off the side of the path. "Hey, Britt. Good girl. Who's a good girl?" She swooned at Olaf's sing-song tone and having her ears tickled.

"So, Claudine and Marc must be around here somewhere or Britt is really lost."

"Well, she can walk with us, if need be, but I hope she hasn't taken a wrong turn somewhere."

"I *did* hear voices before, maybe it was them. Mind you, I can't see anyone around here."

Claudine and Marc were relaxing about 50 metres ahead in a protected natural bunker we couldn't see from the path. Britt had run back to her owners, almost urging us to follow and that's when we found them. They were taking it easy in this ideal spot, treating the day as a rest day, as they were sore and achy from yesterday's trek. Again, it gave me a physical confidence boost to hear I wasn't the only one who was tired and weary from that slog. If this young, obviously fit, duo had found it tough, then I'd managed okay, even if we hadn't tackled the Wainstones. Before we left them, Olaf offered to take their photo.

"Oh, thank you. That is very nice," Claudine said, as Marc proffered his phone. "We have few of them together on this walk; it is either one or other who must take the photograph, so it would be so nice for you to do this."

We'd often found the same thing. Other than selfies, we had very few photos of the two of us because there wasn't always someone else to take a snap. He took three shots, then a quick inspection gave all-smiling approvals and we went on our way. But we had a new-found companion in Britt who wanted to walk with us. Claudine yelled and Marc whistled for her but she strode along, alternating between Olaf's side, then mine, for roughly 100 metres, before Olaf grabbed her collar to spin her back in their direction. Britt had other ideas. Far from the wild dog I'd feared half an hour before, she was now too friendly and wouldn't leave us alone. We stopped, turned around and walked back to where we'd been, with Britt alongside Olaf, until Marc grabbed her collar and headed back to Claudine.

"Thank you, once more," he said, over his shoulder. "Perhaps we'll see you again along the way. Let us hope."

"Yes. Perhaps," Olaf said, with a big tinge of doubt.

The track across the top of the moor meandered towards Tidy

Brown Hill. It had been about four kilometres since Bloworth Crossing and the gradient continued to be kind to my legs which moved more freely than had been the case earlier. My feet, on the other hand, were now a worry so I decided to take a look when we stopped for lunch, which I hoped would be soon. We'd snacked on fruit and chocolate but the cheese was waiting and I was well and truly waiting for it.

We forked off the main track onto Battersby Moor and I saw in the distance a significant-looking monument which I'd somehow only just noticed. A scroll through the guidebook showed it was Cook's Monument, a tribute to the region's most famous son - Captain James Cook - and I suddenly felt a connection to the explorer.

"Ever wondered how different life would be had the Portuguese or Dutch staked their claim on Australia long before Captain Cook?" I asked. "I have. Quite a lot. We'd be way more relaxed but, instead we've had that stiff upper lip, 'Keep Calm and Carry On' outlook. I mean, how good would siestas be? And so suited to our climate."

"I've never really thought about it, to be honest, but I'm all in favour of a siesta. Still, right now, we do need to keep calm and carry on," Olaf said, "because Roseberry Topping still looks a long way away. And what's supposed to happen when we get to Kildale?"

"I'm going to enjoy a Portuguese tart in honour of what might've been." I raised my water bottle in a mock toast but Olaf didn't respond. He was already looking focused as he strode away and I quickly fell into a hypnotic rhythm behind.

Back on track, we soon descended and passed through two gates, not kissing gates this time, much to my disappointment and continued on a sealed road for about a kilometre where the path turned left across a cattle grid. Rock climbers to our right scaled Park Nab, a 15-metre sheer sandstone crag and we stopped to watch them navigate their pulleys, ropes and harnesses. They flung themselves out, jump by jump, before reconnecting with the solid rockface, then once more placed faith in their gear to push off and do it all again. It must be an invigorating pastime but I was glad to have my feet firmly on the ground, even if they were sore. We walked along the levelled-out road, which our knees were thankful for, when a sign indicated Kildale had crept up on us and was now only 500 metres ahead.

It was mid Saturday afternoon and I'd expected the village to be bustling with locals shopping, chatting and walking about, but it was as deserted as a ghost town with no-one to be seen. It made me unsettled and disconcerted, like something had happened and everyone had disappeared (maybe kidnapped by aliens – yes, my mind went there), or perhaps they were simply having an un-British siesta. Then I noticed a small sign spruiking a nearby café and tea garden which led us to the Glebe Cottage Café. Its sun-drenched, gravel courtyard was teeming with people and dogs and was clearly the hub of the village.

As Olaf went inside, I nestled down at a table under a large, shade-giving sycamore and was immediately greeted by three boisterous off-leash dogs. They were clearly looking for a pat or more likely some of our sun-ripening cheese, with their owners oblivious to their antics or whereabouts. I scoured their faces to see if one was Britt, with possibly Claudine and Marc nearby, but a quick inspection showed they were all unfamiliar and, after a quick pat, I shooed them away. Olaf arrived, clearly impressed by the table I'd managed to find.

I mimicked his 'impressed face' at the news he'd ordered coffee and scones, which he knew would make me happy. I was more than happy – I was over the moon – with a need for caffeine and an energy boost to face whatever the afternoon held. I smothered the scone with tangy raspberry jam, then dolloped fresh cream on top and savoured the sweet, fluffy cloud of yumminess. Perfect. It was way better than a Portuguese tart or, dare I say, a vanilla slice.

Sitting comfortably and relaxed in the shade, I suddenly remembered we weren't at the day's end point as Roseberry Topping and our accommodation was still seven kilometres away. My focus all day had been to get to Kildale and I had, mentally and physically, switched off once we'd arrived at the café. With leaden legs, worsening feet and an overall weariness – a cumulative weariness from walking 68 kilometres in four days – I felt incapable of taking another step today. Perhaps my lack of physical preparation was beginning to show and the long-haul nature of a multiday walk was having an impact. Or, maybe I was mentally fatigued from worrying about my physicality. Maybe it was all three but whatever the reason, I couldn't walk the extra distance. I asked Olaf what he wanted to do but he was non-committal and I became frustrated at him for not making the decision. But I knew it was my call. He was letting me walk *my* Cleveland Way and my frustration was selfish and childish. Olaf couldn't have been more supportive or adaptable and I was being a brat.

"Okay, what do you say we get a taxi from here," he said, "we've already walked 16ks and I'd be happy to cab it if you want to."

"Sometimes I swear you can read my mind," I replied, thankful he hadn't.

"Seriously, I'm glad I can't but I can tell you're a bit uptight and pretty much done for the day."

"Yep, you're right on both counts. Taxi it is."

With stiffened muscles, I hobbled into the café to inquire about a taxi and was handed a business card and landline handset; clearly, we weren't the first to have called it a day here.

"Phone reception ain't grand out there," the café owner said. "You'll have more luck if you try in here."

"Oh, thank you so much," I said. "Really appreciate it."

I dialled the number on the card for Stokesley Taxis. When the phone rang out, my heart sank, so I dialled again and, after several more rings, was about to hang up when someone answered. What a relief! But the conversation didn't go well, it was confused and confusing; perhaps my Australian accent was too broad or I spoke too quickly but what I thought was a simple request – to be picked up at the Glebe Cottage Café and taken to the King's Head Inn at Newton-under-Roseberry - was anything but simple. I couldn't make myself understood and needed the café owner's help.

"Aye, here at café, headed for King's Head," he said, repeating what I'd just said. Then, "Aye. Okay then." He hung up looking deflated. "It'll be at least an hour but he's got you on round. Okay?"

"Okay. That's great. Thank you so much. I have no idea what I would've done if we couldn't get a taxi. There's no way I could walk another seven ks today," I replied, not really knowing what being 'on round' meant but grateful we were on it. I still couldn't differentiate between what I'd said and what he'd said but he'd made it happen so that was all that mattered.

Back outside, Olaf had rearranged the seats to spread out and was dozing in the sunshine. He opened an eye as I returned but was happy to continue his kip having been given the lowdown and expected waiting time. I also relaxed in the gentle summer sunshine knowing a hot shower wasn't too far away as more dogs sniffed around and we waited for our silver-coloured saviour to turn up.

It arrived 45 minutes later and I eased my creaking body into the backseat, settled in and watched the North York Moors whizz by, then pass through the village of Easby, and on to Great Ayton with its festooned streets filled with small Australian flags fluttering in the wind.

"In honour of Captain Cook," the driver said, anticipating my question. "He's our favourite son, well our favourite schoolboy, by a country mile. Aye, a country mile." I smiled as I'd come to believe a country mile was quite an arbitrary thing.

We soon arrived at the King's Head Inn, right at the base

of Roseberry Topping, which was conveniently the start of tomorrow's leg. The familiar pyramid shaped landmark now looked steep and rocky up close; its pointy tip a neck-arching 324 metres up, providing a seriously imposing climb to kick us off.

I put that challenging thought aside as we settled into our large double room with windows overlooking an in-bloom cottage garden and started going about our usual end-of-day mundanities. I couldn't wait any longer for a hot, powerful shower and jumped into the bathroom while Olaf was still wringing out his shirt. The unbridled stream of water was so glorious I luxuriated in it for ages (which ordinarily would feel wasteful and come heavy with guilt), but when in Yorkshire, I treated myself and was revived as a result. Emerging from the steamy bathroom, I should've thoroughly inspected my feet but chose to put it off for the time being. Olaf and I touched hands in a tag-team gesture as he took his turn in the shower.

Spruced up and rejuvenated, we headed into the beer garden filled with vibrant, colourful flowerboxes, almost fluorescent in the sunshine and enjoyed a pint of cider and Guinness. More curious dogs came over for a pat (what was with all the dogs today?) or more scrounging for food but quickly disappeared once they realised we didn't have any.

The hotel bustled with weekend walkers, was crowded and noisy and a bit unpleasant. We ate average pub fare then went back to our room and I used this early retreat to send some emails. My parents were eager for news - whether my body was holding up and our likelihood of finishing – so I updated them on our days so far, that I was tired but okay, determined to finish, possibly in a wheelbarrow and knew Mum would disseminate it to extended family members. Another email to my good friend, Susan (giver of the £50 voucher), updated her on the cheese and then my ongoing hair growth. Allison's email had some funny anecdotes and my brother, Warren, received a critique of some local brews. Olaf checked in with our friends looking after our puppy, Maya, then he updated social media to reach a wider group hungry for our news.

With those jobs done, Olaf drew the heavy floral curtains and I slipped under the king-sized bed's sheets and waited for sleep to take hold, trying to put the thought of that steep first-up climb out of my mind, along with the 16.5 kilometres to walk after that. I drifted off in a melange of weariness and concern and an excitement at saying goodbye to the moors and hello to the North Sea coast.

"Sweet ones," Olaf whispered.

MID-TREATMENT GETAWAY

Ninety-four days into treatment, with 68 still to go (yes, I was counting) and I was feeling exhausted to the point where my long-held focus to walk the Cleveland Way was faltering and I started to question if it would happen at all. And Olaf was exhausted as well, at my side every step of the way while juggling the demands of his high-pressure, six-day-a-week job. So, when he suggested a quick weekend getaway in Owen, our VW campervan, I felt like it could be the perfect circuit-breaker to reset and recharge our batteries. Treatment occurred as usual on Friday, along with the weekly heart emoji text from my sister-in-law; vanilla slices with mum were still eaten Saturday morning and Olaf left work early so we could set off just after lunch with a plan to return Monday. I'd organised things, albeit slower than in the past, packed food, organised bedding and gathered some other titbits for the road. We'd heard about a quiet, off-grid, 'free' campground at Narrung, two hours from home on the banks of the Coorong, which sounded perfect and we couldn't wait to relax in the tranquillity.

Almost immediately into the two-hour drive, I started to feel recharged. It was like the black cape of our medically imposed routine was temporarily thrown off and our lighter, familiar connection was being allowed to flourish. But as we neared our secluded, serene spot, all hopes of it being quiet were smashed and our naivety blatantly obvious. It was a long weekend and the perfect early autumn weather meant campers of all descriptions shared the same idea as us. Caravans, tents, camper trailers and motorhomes were in every tight space along the waterfront with no room anywhere for us. It wasn't at all what we'd envisaged, in fact, the polar opposite and we had to decide if we'd turn around and go home or try and find another campground (potentially with the same outcome). But when Olaf discovered a hidden, just-big-enough space for Owen to squeeze into, the decision was made to stay. He carefully manoeuvred the van back and forth as I breathed-in to 'help' fit. We levelled the tyres, popped up the roof and about 15 minutes later, were sitting under the awning enjoying a drink and some crisps in the golden mid-afternoon sunshine.

"Hey there, folks!" yelled a man exiting a caravan next door.

"Ah, g'day mate," replied Olaf, in a greeting I'd rarely heard from him.

"Got a good set-up there, mate. How long you had it?" He was walking over with a beer in one hand and a cigarette in the other.

"A couple of years and we love it," Olaf said. "We can pull up and be set up within minutes as you probably just saw. It's great."

"She looks a beauty, mate. Much room inside?" His head was already crooked around the door. This seemed to happen all the time on our road trips, which I found intrusive but able to accept, however, I couldn't accept it this time. I wanted solitude, time to reflect and reset and I wanted him to leave immediately. He clearly didn't pick up on my thoughts as his focus turned to me.

"Looks like you're having a rough trot at the minute, love."

"Yeah. It's not much fun," I said, not wanting to engage.

"Breast cancer? If you don't mind me asking."

"Yep," I said, but I *did* mind. I probably seemed rude or abrupt, but his question had taken me aback, not just with its forthrightness, but I thought I looked inconspicuous. My sunhat masked my baldness and sunglasses covered 'missing' eyebrows. I thought no-one could tell I was having chemotherapy unless they took a long and very hard look. But he'd scarcely even glanced at me, seeming much more interested in Olaf and the van, yet seen straight through my 'camouflage'. I really, really wanted him to go now and leave us alone.

"You're very brave," he said. "How much more treatment have you got to go?"

"Ten weeks." I smiled but teared up behind my sunnies. I really wanted this man, who'd made me realise I *did* look like someone with cancer, to go as far away as possible. NOW!

"Well, you know what they say, love - tough times don't last but tough people do."

I couldn't respond. He was showing me kindness and all I wanted was for him to go away. It wasn't his fault. I'd been delusional about how I looked, how I'd tried to be brave in the face of people's judgement, that I was sick and tired of feeling sick and tired. He was being a good person and I was wallowing in the mire of self-pity. Why did I react like this when people offered compassion?

Olaf broke the awkward silence.

"We just wanted to come away, relax and get off the treatment treadmill for a bit, but it's much busier than we expected."

"Yeah. Long weekends are always busy here," he said.

"Anyway, we're going to make the most of our 'away' time together."

"Yep. Right-o. Leave you to it. If there's anything you need, let me know."

"That's very kind, thank you," I managed. It *was* very kind.

"Good luck with the next 10 weeks, love. And after that

too, of course. You're simply amazing. God bless you." He'd finished his beer and cigarette and walked back towards his van.

I retreated into the safety of Owen feeling exposed and vulnerable and immediately burst into tears. Those tears turned into a gushing torrent accompanied by uncontrollable guttural moans. Olaf didn't know what had happened but protectively held me as months of built-up emotions released, until gradually the reservoir of tears ran dry and we lay down exhausted.

The next day was spent driving around the Lower Lakes, enjoying a couple of short walks (no long-distance hikes were possible right now), enjoying the sunshine and a French-style picnic of bread and cheese. The good cry the day before had been a huge release and helped me positively face the next part of my journey. My attitude would play a big part in whether we'd get to Helmsley to start our 175-kilometre walk in a few months and I knew negative thoughts, including resenting someone for being kind, was no way to live. As we drove back to the campground, I felt an unusual calmness and vowed to be more gracious towards our neighbour should we see him again.

We'd no sooner arrived and set ourselves up when he strolled over to ask about our day. I still wasn't overjoyed by his presence but wasn't annoyed, angry or upset like the day before. He chatted for no more than five minutes, almost like a custodian of the park welcoming us back and I was glad of my new approach to offer an open heart.

The night rolled in; we ate dinner then snuggled inside our home away from home for an early night. But I was unaware that as I'd cooked dinner, Olaf had posted photos of our day, of me uncovered, of me clearly mid-treatment, on social media. It prompted a second outpouring of concern and support from people who didn't know of my situation, so when our phones pinged with messages of shock, love and hope, it hit me again like a tidal wave. But it somehow felt different this time. It was still overwhelming and a lot to accept, but I felt better equipped to receive it. So, when a dear friend sent the message, *I know we haven't caught up for a while, but you've either had a serious conversion to Buddhism or you're going through a tough time,* all I could do was laugh. Something had clearly shifted in me, in no small part thanks to our 'nosy caravan neighbour' who'd woken me up to my subconscious resistance to kindness, to my initial protective response to avoid acknowledging my cancer was real. Well, it was real, it was very real and accepting all the love on offer was the best and only way forward.

The weekend was invaluable. I came home feeling different, unburdened and many shades lighter than when I'd left two days before. The release of pent-up emotions, the realisation I'd been shutting out love and care (even from strangers) and a renewed focus beyond the next 10 weeks had shaken me from my protective bubble and would hopefully help me through the inevitable tough days to come. But there was one nagging thing I really wanted to do; I called that caring distant friend who I'd ignored months ago and told her how I was and how much I appreciated her support. We discussed all manner of things but neither of us mentioned, let alone insisted on, chatting with her friend, as she had suggested. Perhaps we'd both had a chance to reflect and consider each other's needs. I certainly had.

Day 5
ROSEBERRY TOPPING TO
SALTBURN-BY-THE-SEA
14.5 kilometres

The curtains succeeded in keeping the room dark, but the morning light pushed its way through the small gap, cleaving the millimetre of space between the drawn fabric. Funnily, on a normal working morning when my alarm jolts me awake at 5:45am I'm resentful of it and often don't want to get up, but on days like today when I'm naturally awake at that time, with no urgency to rise, it feels completely different, yet it's the same amount of sleep. I enjoyed not having to get up yet and was blissfully relaxed.

Olaf's breath was rhythmic and soothing; he was clearly unaffected by the ever-increasing volume of the avian chorus outside and I continued to absorb the moment. I nestled in beside him as my jukebox silently played a line from the Split Enz song, *Message to My Girl* – *No-one else can touch us, while we're in this place*. We lay like that for another 20 minutes as I soaked in the safety and security he offered, even while he slept. If we had each other – we had everything.

"Oh, shit! Shit, shit, shit," I yelled, sitting bolt upright.

"What's the matter? You okay?" Olaf asked.

"Cramp in my calf. Oh, God. Can you push my toes back? NOW!"

"Yep." He pushed and the spasm immediately ceased.

"Geez, that was painful. Actually, it still is." I kept stretching. "Mustn't have had enough water."

"Maybe. Or it could be that you just finished chemo and have walked nearly 70ks in four days. That could have something to do with it."

"Yeah. Nah. I didn't drink enough water. I'll have to make sure I do today." I'd deflected Olaf's comment, but he was probably right. My single-minded determination to finish this walk had left little room to reflect on the battering my body was taking.

"Right. Well, I'll fill the water bottles while you sort the food. There's still a bit of cheese to get through by the looks."

"We're going okay. We've finished the softer ones but still got these big chunks of cheddar, so don't panic, our supplies are good. I love how this has become part of our walk. Not many people would carry all this cheese with them. In fact, I'm pretty sure nobody would."

"I like it too. Just maybe not as much as you, Minnie. Hey, don't forget we'll see the coast today. That'll be exciting."

"It'll be a nice change, going from the moors to the sea. More to see – I like that."

"Change of scenery and all that. But there's still a bit of walking to do before we get there, starting with that climb right there."

"Mmmmmm. And it'll probably be crowded given all the people around the place."

My calf still smarted as I assessed my feet, wondering if my big toe needed proper medical attention to avoid becoming infected. It was red and raw and very tender but I'd managed to keep it clean so far. I'd see how it held up today. I popped the blisters on my other heel with a disinfected safety pin, gave them extra swabbing and padding and hoped that would suffice. A thin layer of Vaseline was rubbed around each stained toenail bed and the big nails were wrapped in bandaging which seemed to hold them together. I dove my feet into my socks and tried not to wince as I tied my shoelaces. Olaf buttoned up his shirt without saying a word.

Fifteen minutes later, our bags were ready for collection, water bottles packed, along with some Montgomery's Cheddar and this well-organised routine meant we were the first hotel guests looking for breakfast.

I was already on my second coffee when the scrambled eggs and bacon arrived. The dining area was filling and with it a gentle buzz of conversation. It looked like everyone was there to scale the 320-metre Roseberry Topping and a quick glance around revealed the diversity of climbers. Families with young children, serious-looking walkers, an older couple and other inappropriately dressed patrons, all appeared to have the same goal.

Only two days ago we'd noticed a little wedge on the horizon which looked half a world away, now here we were about to tackle it and possibly tackle some fellow breakfasters as well. I scrolled back through our photos to check how far we'd come and the confirmation we'd covered a fair whack of ground gave me a surge of motivation for the day's task ahead – a 14.5-kilometre walk across the moors, through forest and farmland, then finishing at the North Sea.

Keen to set off before the disparate hordes, we finished eating, checked out, slung on our backpacks and headed through the beer garden to join the path leading to 'Yorkshire's Matterhorn'. As we neared the base, I knew I'd underestimated its size and definitely its gradient, along with the large, stone steps requiring a step ladder to climb. After 15 of these oversized, giant steps, my thigh muscles were already screaming and I foolishly looked up.

"I can't do this," I shouted to Olaf, but he was already way ahead and continuing to climb. "I don't think I can do this," I yelled louder, determined to make him hear.

I stopped for a breather, feeling deflated at scarcely having left the ground, with no idea if I could get to the top. I was on the edge of tears when an unfit man wearing ill-fitting jeans and thongs skipped up the enormous steps beside me. He nodded as he passed, then exhaled cigarette smoke which blew straight into my face. I spluttered, annoyed and taken aback, but it spurred me into action - if this bogan Puffing Billy could make it to the top, so could I. I looked up again and Olaf had stopped, still a long way ahead, waiting for me to catch up.

"Okay. Let's think about this," he said, "we can go back down and get a taxi or we can take this one slow step at a time and see how we go. What do you want to do?"

"I don't want to go back down but I don't know how I can possibly get up there. My legs are already like jelly."

"Right. So, we're continuing on. Good. And we can stop whenever we want. Remember, there are no prizes riding on this."

"Yep, I know. Did you see that bloke wearing thongs zoom straight past me and he was smoking? Didn't look like he could climb anything but he's probably at the top by now."

"You're stalling. Come on, get those jelly legs moving and we'll be there soon enough. Promise."

I groaned as I climbed the next step, then again on the one after that, but slowly my legs loosened, the caffeine kicked in and a gradual physical confidence came with it. More weekenders overtook us but I mustered strength from somewhere and before I knew it, we were approaching the top third of the climb and, despite what Olaf had said, there *was* a prize at the end of this - reaching the top and overcoming my mental hurdles would be my prize, regardless of how long it took or who else was doing it. I put my head down and bum up, pushing my legs to climb, climb, climb the remainder of the nuggety path.

I stopped twice to catch my breath and rest my lactic legs and then found ourselves at the final escarpment. Some careful foot placement ensured I didn't slip and, with a bit of scrambling, we reached the summit and the symbolic cairn which had a cartoon sheep, possibly Shaun the Sheep, drawn on its white surface. I let out a combined laugh and sigh as we touched the strived-for monument. What seemed improbable had now been achieved, even if my jelly-like legs couldn't stop trembling. And there was my prize, the 360-degree views across Yorkshire, south to the Cleveland Hills and north-east to the coast, received as a wave of satisfaction crashed in and emotions spilled out. There were times during chemo, feeling nauseous and fatigued, when this moment seemed more than a million miles away. I couldn't see how I'd be strong enough to do anything close to this and then I remembered that prophetic phrase: *You might surprise yourself how well you'll come through all this.* Right then, I was very surprised and very proud but there was still a long way to go.

Olaf enveloped me in his arms and I wanted to freeze time forever. But then a woman bobbed up from nowhere and offered to take our photo – an offer we didn't want to refuse – so I blew my nose, wiped my eyes, leant in to Olaf and gave her a big-toothed smile. Olaf took her photo in return; we chatted for a few minutes before she scampered on her way down the other side.

It was an emotional circuit-breaker for me and meant I could refocus on the day's still-lengthy walk. My legs had settled, although my left calf still gave an occasional reminder to keep my fluids up, so we had a quick slug of water under the overcast skies. There were still 14 kilometres before we made the coast and, as satisfying as this achievement was, we needed to keep moving. My first challenge for the day had been ticked off, now for the forest and beyond.

The descent had more steep, winding steps and I worried about Olaf's knee. He assured me he was okay but I could tell he was in a degree of pain. Two chatting and giggling children, aged 11 or 12, whizzed past leaving us completely in their wake and I decided the 'speedy' couple from two days ago were probably like that as youngsters.

In our tortoise-like fashion, we got to the bottom then traipsed across open grassland heading to Guisborough Woods. We walked along a wide, bracken-lined track, before reaching a gate sporting a Cleveland Way sign.

"This is where we would've walked to if we hadn't got that taxi yesterday," Olaf said.

"Hang on, I'm confused. Let me think about this. That means if we'd walked the extra seven ks from Kildale, we'd have ended up here. Which means we would've gone up Roseberry Topping from this side, then down the other side to get to our hotel. Then this morning we would've had to do what we've just done to get here and back onto the path."

"Yep. That's exactly what it means."

"So, basically, we would've climbed it twice. Not that I doubted it, but I knew that taxi was a good idea."

"Me too. It was an excellent idea, if I do say so myself. Maybe now my knee might last the rest of the walk."

"It's sore, isn't it? You are limping a bit."

"Nah. It's fine. I'll be right. Just getting extra good mileage out of it."

So, catching that taxi hadn't signified failure; it had been a smart decision, which gave us the best chance of finishing the walk.

Back on the official path, we headed east for half a kilometre alongside a plantation, then turned right and followed a stone boundary wall while in the distance horses grazed around Highcliff Farm. I hurried ahead, having seen the kissing gate before Olaf, quickly weaved through, closed my eyes and turned with puckered lips. But when I opened my eyes, it wasn't Olaf standing in front of me, it was an unknown man with a look of horror on his face. He must've approached from the other direction and snuck up at the last minute. I was totally stunned, very embarrassed and apologised to the petrified stranger as I opened the gate to let him through (without adhering to our strict rules). He took off in haste, muttering something under his breath.

"Where the hell did he come from?" Olaf asked, chuckling.

"Absolutely no idea. People seem to bob-up out of nowhere around here." After a quick double-check I puckered up again, then allowed Olaf through the gate vowing to expand my peripheral vision from now on.

Still chuckling, we returned to our walking rhythm before veering right and crossing a forest track. We followed a narrow walkway around the base of a hill where our guidebook urged us to 'follow signs carefully'. That set alarm bells ringing in my head and I would be even more vigilant about following the instructions.

The steep climb up rocky steps led to the top of the yellow-faced Highcliff Nab with a new vista overlooking the large market town of Guisborough. We continued along the escarpment's edge, checking the instructions with almost every step, then headed into a woodland of spruce and conifer.

At the first track junction go straight ahead; at the second junction fork left downhill. There was nothing complicated about these instructions, but as we went further into the forest I became more and more unsure. Maybe it was the warning to be careful that made me wary or perhaps my intuition had kicked in and I sensed something wasn't right. The trees became denser, which meant less light and was more slippery, so my walking pole steadied each foot placement, putting one carefully in front of the other. At the first track junction we continued straight ahead, confident we were on the right track and my earlier anxiety started to lift. Then as we approached the second junction it returned and I frantically referred to the guidebook.

"We have to fork left downhill," I insisted, raising the book.

"But take a look at this," Olaf said. He was pointing to a signpost with a thick, black, hand-drawn arrow pointing to the right. "It looks recent, and whoever did it has gone to a lot of trouble to point us that way; I assume for good reason."

But the guidebook had warned to 'follow signs carefully', and I wasn't sure what to do.

"So, you think we should go that way. What if it's a prank? The instructions clearly say go this way." Then I tried to lighten the mood by quoting Olaf's favourite literary character. "I think we need to do a Jack Reacher, *If in doubt - turn left!*" But he wasn't amused. He wanted to follow the arrow markings of Mr or Mrs Anonymous, rather than those in our published directions. He could see I didn't agree.

"Okay. We'll take the left path and just hope Reacher doesn't let us down," he said.

The left path *did* slope gently downhill and we strode in a tense silence, unsure how our decision would play out. It would either be a moment of, 'All hail, Jack Reacher' or 'I knew we should've gone the other way', but for now, there was a quiet unease not knowing which one of us was right. We walked for five minutes looking out for another track to cross but, after another kilometre with no track, I scoured the guidebook in an attempt to match-up our surroundings. But there were no landmarks, no way-markers, just muddy paths and row after identical row of pine trees. We kept walking and I hoped something would appear to confirm we were on the right track but I knew we were lost.

"I told you we should've gone the other way," Olaf said. "Someone else must've made this mistake and was trying to warn us." I went to reply but had nothing to add. "Well, we might as well find somewhere to have lunch and then try and work out where the hell we are."

"Yep. Okay." It was all I could manage.

It had already been a physically challenging day. I was hungry, tired and now we were lost. The logical side of my brain had switched off and my bottom lip quivered as a petulant reaction to our predicament.

"Bloody Reacher!" Olaf said. "I think we need a new mantra – that last one didn't go so well."

"My daily recital, *Wellness is the natural state of my body*, isn't going to do much for us right now, is it?"

"Nope. What about - *If in doubt, eat cheese*?" Olaf said. "It's not something Reacher would say but at least we can't go wrong."

"You always say the right things. Montgomery's Cheddar coming up - perfect for when you're lost in a forest."

"I don't think they'll be adopting that slogan any time soon."

I offloaded my pack, which lifted a weight from my shoulders, both literally and metaphorically. Olaf found a dry, solid spot to sit and we made a concerted effort to rehydrate. It was only a short break but made all the difference to my attitude to the point where I was almost able to enjoy the idyllic surrounds. Well, it would've been idyllic if we weren't lost, but I could still manage to appreciate nature's beauty. It seemed like days since we'd climbed Roseberry Topping, not just a few hours, and we'd soon be arriving at the coast - if we could just find a way out of the forest. But all I could see were more trees.

"I think it's being in the northern hemisphere," I said, "I have no sense of north or south and it's easy to get lost."

"Maybe. Or perhaps we should've turned right back there," Olaf replied.

"You're really pissed off about that, aren't you?"

"Yep."

"So, do we keep going, or what do you want to do?"

"Might as well keep going and if we can't work out where we are, I'll see if I can get a signal for my phone's GPS to get us out of here."

We'd gone a few hundred metres when a young boy and a teenage girl climbed out of a thicket about 20 metres ahead and were walking our way.

"Do you happen to know where the Cleveland Way is?" Olaf asked, as they neared.

"Nup. Never heard of it," the girl replied as she shook her head, before they disappeared into the forest on the other side of our makeshift path.

Rather than being deflated by this brief, dismissive encounter, I was buoyed at seeing other people, so maybe we weren't quite as lost as I'd thought. We continued looking for landmarks to help navigate through the thick fernlike undergrowth but there was nothing to assist, so Olaf grabbed his phone. Bingo! He had a very weak signal and his GPS led us up a steep path in the opposite direction to that of my internal compass. Having already led us astray once, I decided to follow another piece of Reacher's advice, *If in doubt, say nothing,* so I silently followed Olaf, sure we were doubling back on ourselves, heading deeper into the forest for about a kilometre.

"Do you reckon this counts as a dilapidated estate wall?" I asked, checking the guidebook yet again.

"Yes, I do. And doesn't it say something about that village in the distance too?" It could be seen through a large gap in the trees.

"Yes, it does! It does!"

"Well, I think we might be back on track."

It was a relief to see a way-marker confirm we were officially back on the Cleveland Way. Thank goodness for that weak signal popping up and for Olaf's GPS. My stride became spritely and I'd completely forgotten about my patched-up feet and sore muscles. With focus and direction, we walked along the forest's edge, crossed a gully, turned onto a joint-jarring concrete drive, took a sharp right onto a narrow path, then into a broad, well-signed woodland. Then, scaring the hell out of us, several off-road motorbikes roared up from behind, crisscrossed our path at speed and had no regard for anyone unlucky enough to be in their way. The chainsaw-like pitch pierced our eardrums and, for a moment, I thought about heading back into the forest but there was a coastline waiting for our arrival.

We had to be super alert to these weekend warriors - I assumed Sunday was one of the track's busier days – but the aural assault left us in no doubt as to when they were approaching. We choreographed our way through narrow gates and along a fence-line to avoid being skittled, until the path came out alongside the busy A171 motorway where trucks, cars and buses whizzed by. We caught our breath and waited for the traffic to break long enough to scurry across safely. My heart rate was pounding and my legs were like jelly but we were now out of the woods – finally.

A few more deep breaths then our walk continued past the enticing Fox and Hounds pub, behind some houses, then up a very steep flight of steps. If my legs could talk, they would've screamed, *You cannot be serious!* but the path soon levelled out and, ta-da – we could see the coastline. The diversity of the moorland had been beautiful and was, at that moment, behind us so my focus could now turn to new panoramas and a different type of path. It was going to be a whole new experience in Part Two of the Cleveland Way.

A sign for the next village of Skelton Green showed it was three kilometres away as another steep path levelled out. Contented cows grazed in pastures and basked in the afternoon warmth and I took Olaf's hand as we walked side by side for a kilometre or so. It was the home stretch of a very diverse day and, as we approached Skelton Green, suddenly nature urgently called. I couldn't wait. I needed to use the facilities of the pub we were walking past, even though our day's walk was nearly over. I practically ran into the Green Inn and Olaf followed slowly behind.

"Fancy a cider?" Olaf asked, as I joined him at the table where he'd made himself comfortable.

I hesitated, noticing a bottle of Cleveland Way gin and momentarily considered the local drop. But that would be for another time.

"Hell, yes. Why not? And a packet of crisps."

One cider became two in the slightly rundown, dour surrounds but some jovial banter with three, elderly local men made for a light and spirited break. Feeling revitalised, we almost skipped down the steps towards Skelton High Street, then downhill along Derwent Road where a sign for Saltburn showed – 1.5 kilometres to go. Nearly there.

We descended into the Saltburn Valley, walked through an underpass under the A174 and entered a magical wooded gorge towered over by a 55-metre high, red-brick railway viaduct spanning the expanse with its 11 arches.

"Wow! Those arches are beautiful. Almost sculptural," I said.

"Geez. How on earth would they have built it? It's a frigging long way up there," said Olaf.

"I don't know but the guidebook barely gives it a mention. I was definitely not expecting that."

"No. Me either. I wonder if it's still used."

I doubted it was still in use as, up close, it was obvious the 150-year-old Saltburn Viaduct needed a lot of maintenance but I hoped a train might come over and prove me wrong. We walked on, unable to take our eyes off it, clearly having different thoughts as we went: me about its beauty, Olaf its engineering, but we were united in our admiration of its presence.

Then it was uphill once more and a strong wind welcomed us to the coast as we walked past the Saltburn Valley Gardens. A brass band was playing which added a jaunty Sunday afternoon ambience to this arts-inspired village with its grand, Victorian architecture. As we continued past a playground, the road flattened out and provided wonderful views – south to the jagged coastal cliffs, and north to the 27-turbine, offshore Redcar Wind Farm which looked to be levitating in the North Sea. The slow-turning blades synchronising to create 62 megawatts of renewable power.

We headed towards the Spa Hotel, our accommodation for the night, which sat atop the seafront overlooking the 150-year-old pier and funicular cliff lift. We checked in and, within minutes, I was soaking in a luxurious, deep bath. It was heaven and I didn't move for at least 20 minutes, reflecting on the spectrum of the day's events: starting with that climb, getting lost, dodging dirt bikes, having ciders with locals and now we were at the sea. So many experiences in just a few hours. *This* was why I loved walking holidays, *this* was what had kept me focused, *this* was how nature worked its magic. What a story it would make. I washed away the more challenging parts of the day and soaked in the triumph of simply being here as the seed of an idea sprouted. I'd let it germinate over the next few days and see if it might grow.

"Better get this washed so it has a chance to dry," Olaf said bursting in, holding up his trusty shirt. "You look comfy in there."

"It's so good. I *do* love a bath, particularly after a day like today. My legs will be stiff tomorrow I can already tell."

"If only we'd brought G with us to work her magic on our muscles. Actually, magic isn't the right word, more like inflict pain." Our friend G, short for Giovanna, was also our kind and generous massage therapist who'd kneaded and rubbed our bodies for years. We often joked that her idea of fun was to make grown women and men cry even if her gentle soul and warm exterior belied that idea.

"Oh God! She would pummel us into submission but it would be so good, once it was over."

"Are you going wrinkly yet? You've been in there a while. Not that there's any rush to get out."

"I've got wrinkly fingers, yes. It's been very therapeutic and quite productive."

"That's good. Productive? That explains the look on your face. I'm not going to ask – sometimes it's best not to. What I will ask though is, do you think this is properly clean? I thought it was a bit smelly today." He held up his wringing wet shirt.

"It looks clean and I didn't smell it today. But maybe you could wear a different shirt tomorrow."

"Ha! Good one. That's not going to happen."

I dried and caught a glimpse of myself in the mirror and was shocked and delighted to see how much my hair had grown. It had started to sprout from other parts of my body as well. Yes, I'd lost it everywhere, not just my head and I startled Olaf as I yelped in delight. The days of physical exertion must've acted like a turbocharger for healing. I then saw that my stained *smoker* fingernails had also had a growth spurt and I'd soon be able to start cutting away the awful brown blemish. Things were looking up. Then I glanced down at my feet, hoping they'd joined in on the recovery wave but the blisters were still red and raw and the bunions flaring red. But on closer inspection, my toenails definitely weren't as chalky as they had been and had also grown a little. I felt I could start expunging their brown bloom pretty soon. I was inspired to see signs of healing, obvious, tangible signs, and I couldn't wait to see what else might happen over the next four days of walking.

Once Olaf had showered and hung-up various bits of hand-washed laundry, we headed to the restaurant to enjoy a Sunday roast overlooking the choppy water. That strong coastal wind had picked up, along with the chill factor and merrymakers basking on the outside deck were forced inside to shelter. I'd hoped the coast might be friendlier than the moors but it looked like the wind could be an unpleasant antagonist. Still, I was confident the worst of the climbing was behind us even though tomorrow's section, Saltburn to Sandsend, a whopping 27.5 kilometres, promised undulations and steep gradients.

We needed an early night given the length of tomorrow's walk and were back in our room with plenty of time to load the packs in readiness for an early start. Olaf immediately checked our washed clothes then settled into a Sudoku. I filled our water bottles then dived into our cheese stash, where we now only had two still-wrapped chunks left and I made a mental note to 'get' some fruit at breakfast to top up our snacks.

"God, I hate that!" Olaf said. "I made a mistake and don't know where."

"It's funny how you get so annoyed by a boo-boo in Sudoku but not by other way more frustrating things."

"That's because there isn't anything more frustrating than this."

"No. Nothing. Like getting lost in a forest or anything."

"Don't get me started on that. We should've taken the right turn."

WHY DID I GET CANCER?

"Is there a history of breast cancer in your family?" my oncologist asked as one of his first questions.

"No. I've always felt lucky about that. There's no history in our family," I replied.

"Mmmmm. Okay. Are you sure about that?" His hushed tones were challenging.

"Yes. Well, I can't be absolutely sure going back before my grandmothers, but as far as I know, there's no family history."

"Okay. That's interesting and unusual." He paused then added, "How would you feel about genetic testing to find out? I think it would be beneficial."

"Oh. I don't know. I'd have to give it some thought. How would it be beneficial?"

"Well, it could inform future treatment and, of course, would help your relatives. Anyway, give it some thought, you don't have to decide straight away. I'll refer you to the Genetics Unit who'll make contact but it's your decision."

Did I want to know or not? Was my cancer caused by a predetermined genetic timebomb I was helpless to defuse? And how would finding out impact my outlook? In one sense, at least it could explain why I got cancer and, if I did have the BRCA gene, it would direct any decisions about my left breast. But if the test came back negative, that question of 'why did I get cancer?' would still remain.

I'd asked myself that question over and over but knew there was no definitive answer. There was plenty to speculate on and many people had - was it using HRT after the hysterectomy, or having taken the contraceptive pill for years? Maybe it was having a high-stress job with a narcissistic manager – had that caused it? Had I suppressed too many emotions or anger? Then there was the guilt of enjoying a few glasses of wine (or cider) and eating meat or cheese, enjoying a little sugar – was all that to blame? It had been suggested, as I'd not had children and not breastfed, that may have been the cause. Everyone had their opinion. Had I, in essence, as one relative hurtfully said, somehow brought the disease on myself?

A few weeks later, a package from the Genetics Unit arrived with reams of information about the testing process, its implications and the next steps should I go ahead. A session with a genetics counsellor was offered and I figured there was no harm in taking it up. There was no obligation, no pressure, just an hour-long chat to hopefully provide clarity around this process.

"There's no rush to make a decision; you can take as long as you need," she said. "If you come back in six months, 12 months or two years wanting the test, that's completely fine. But to be honest, I reckon after two years, you've probably decided *not* to go ahead which again is completely fine."

"What would *you* do if you were in this position?" I asked.

"With my geneticist hat on, I'd say if taking a test can prevent or minimise disease at all, I'd definitely do it. But from a personal point of view, if it was testing for something incurable, like Alzheimer's, for example, I really wouldn't want to know. That probably doesn't help you much, does it?"

"It does, sort of, I think. It's all been such a whirlwind; I just need to get my head around what it means before I can decide."

"Take as long as you need, there's no rush - it's your decision either way."

Some friends and family thought it a no-brainer - of course you'd want to know and take back control and stop wondering. For others, the emotional impact was obvious and the decision not so clear-cut. I wavered somewhere between the two. Olaf left it up to me, saying only I could make the decision but, of course, he supported whichever way I went. And so, for a while, I put it in the too hard basket, pushed it to one side for a few months and got on with healing.

Until the day my sister called to share her dreaded news. Allison moved her regular mammogram forward several months, just for peace of mind, but as she started to share her experience I broke into a sweat. I was back in that airless room, reliving the anxiety of knowing something wasn't right. She had more scans, then a biopsy, then was delivered the awful blow. She had a ductal carcinoma in situ or DCIS. It was the smallest of tumours, in its early infancy, but it was breast cancer, nonetheless.

As she spoke, I felt every emotion with her, then felt overwhelmed with guilt. I knew I hadn't given her cancer but somehow felt responsible. We'd shared so much in the past: clothes, secrets, a bedroom, the joys of her three pregnancies but this was one life experience I didn't want us to share. It was one thing for me to go through this but she shouldn't have to as well. She'd already had one life-threatening illness, a brain aneurysm in her 20s and didn't deserve this now. That near-death experience took years of recovery, conquering partial vision loss, physical ailments and tackling speech issues, so I knew she could handle whatever lay ahead but it just didn't seem fair.

"Thank you," she said. "Thank you."

"What for? I feel like it's all my fault even though I know it can't be."

"Exactly – it can't be. It's the opposite to being your fault. If you hadn't nagged me to move the scan, well, let's not even think about it. You've probably saved my life."

"I don't feel like a life saver right now, I actually feel sick."

Within days, she'd had minor excision surgery and avoided any radiation, chemotherapy or ongoing medication, all because it had been detected so early. And, as she pondered the same 'why me' question, I knew genetic testing wasn't just about me anymore – the choice was now clear.

When the call came to find out the result, my anxiety levels skyrocketed and I was glad the geneticist cut to the chase.

"I've got your results," she said, as I consciously slowed my breathing.

"Oh, wow! Okay," I said, as I felt my heart thumping.

"How are you feeling? Are you okay?"

"Um. I'm a bit numb to be honest. I didn't think I'd be this emotional. But it's better to know."

"Well, it is a big thing. You've been brave."

She listed the detailed results which I vaguely took in, made sure I was okay, then wished me luck in the future. And that was that - test done, result known. No BRCA genes. The relief took me by surprise but knowing I wasn't predisposed to genetically mutate was a big thing. Perhaps if the result was different, I may have felt otherwise, but the negative finding meant it was situation normal (well, as normal as could be) and a relief for Allison and the other women in my family. And, as for the ongoing mystery as to why I got cancer, as my surgeon said, "If I knew that, I'd have 10 Nobel Prizes."

Day 6
SALTBURN-BY-THE-SEA TO SANDSEND
27.5 kilometres

We sluggishly made our way to breakfast, having finished our well-oiled morning routine almost in our sleep. Our luggage was ready to be collected, the backpacks 90% stocked, with just a few last-minute things to do before we were on our way along the coast. The most important of which was bandaging my worsening feet. We opted for a lighter meal and two rounds of coffee, the caffeine helping to boost my energy and stamina, and I was excited by the prospect of today's new terrain. But being the longest leg on the Cleveland Way also meant I was apprehensive and nervous about my heavy, weary legs. The cumulative effect of five days back-to-back walking was obvious and it wasn't even the 'big' muscles that hurt, it was the little ones around the knees, those 'braking' muscles needed when travelling downhill and the little ankle stabilisers which pinged with each step. But with no Roseberry Topping to scale, no pine forests to get lost in and no seemingly endless stone walls to worry about, the day *should* go without a hitch.

I finished the cup and headed back to our room, taking some pears I'd tucked in my jacket, to tick off those final tasks before setting off southward on the cool, overcast morning. My sad feet needed attention and, although the nails seemed to be staying solid(ish), the blisters were raw and my right little toe had joined in as well. With some delicate and painful dabbing and plastering, then careful insertion into socks and shoes, I hoped they would survive the imminent pounding. However, with today the equivalent length of two days in one, it was going to be a challenge. I'd check them at Staithes over lunch, when I assessed the rest of my body. Now I was ready to greet the North Sea but noticed Olaf was moving slower than usual. I saw him wince as he quietly rubbed anti-inflammatory cream into his worn-out knee. He didn't mention it but was clearly struggling with the pain.

Any hope of easing my legs into the day went straight out the window as we set off past some beached boats. Even though I knew what to expect, starting each day didn't get any easier. It was a bit like holding a yin yoga pose where, in the beginning, your body screams and your mind rattles around but then, in some alchemic moment a few minutes in, everything releases and magically moves to a different level. I'd practised yoga on and off since I was a teenager, loving its mind – and soul-enriching benefits along with the physical prowess it required and I'd roped Olaf into joining me over the last three years. It was his first crack at it, having assumed it was too passive for a fit, active man and he immediately embraced it. In fact, he would tell anyone who would listen about his improved flexibility, better core strength and greater capacity to unwind. He was a convert and we were committed yogis. But my attendance at class was paused following the mastectomy and Olaf, after a couple of times on his own, stopped going as well. Through the months of chemo, I willed myself to go, knowing a gentle practice would fill my spiritual cup but there was underlying resistance and the effort was just too great. We'd definitely get back into it when the time was right.

Today, it was just a matter of my muscles getting through that initial 'screaming and rattling' and emerging into a smooth walking rhythm. I hoped that would happen sooner rather than later but had to accept there was no forcing it. Then, to add to my equally divided mental and muscular struggle, we faced a seriously steep climb up some steps behind the ancient Ship Inn. A memorial at the base alluded to a young man's suicide from the clifftops above and it seemed to compound my body's heaviness as we slowly rose from sea level to above Saltburn Scar. I stopped to catch my breath but tried to give the impression I was looking back at the village and nearby balletic wind farm.

"What a great view," I said trying not to puff. "Such a gorgeous contrast of old and new."

"It's gotta be seriously deep out there. I wonder how they built it," Olaf said, always wondering about something.

So, situation normal – me admiring the beauty as Olaf pondered the engineering. But what wasn't normal was he didn't seem overly eager to move on. We turned around after a few moments to head south again and noticed a monument, exactly like the one at the start of the route, this time carved with *Cleveland Coast*, defaced by graffiti scribbled across its façade. A few metres along was a bunch of fresh flowers and a note laid on the cliff's edge. It was a tribute to that young man whose life was lost right at that spot and again, it was like a weight blanketed me as we stood and took in the situation. I rolled the acorn in my pocket between my thumb and fingers, as I'd seen people do with rosary beads, thinking of his troubled soul. Then, much to my horror, Olaf tentatively stepped to peek over the edge.

"What are you doing?" I yelled. "Don't get too close."

He quickly stepped back as the frailty of the rockface became clear and the severity of the drop revealed itself.

"What a horrible way to go," he said.

"Please don't do that. It gives me the heebie-jeebies."

"I honestly don't understand why you'd choose to go like that. Don't worry, I will stay well clear now. It *is* quite precarious."

"Good. I mean, it's just that you've got the cheese in there and if that went over, I'd have no snacks." I tried to lighten the mood, but I hated him getting that close. "Hey, look at that," I said pointing inland to the horizon on our right, "I can't believe we started there yesterday."

The tiny pyramid shape was way off in the distance and we were looking at Roseberry Topping from the other side. It was so far away, yet we'd climbed it only yesterday.

"Wow. Amazing how much ground you can cover in such a short time."

At least it wasn't his usual, *One foot in front of the other* mantra I'd expected but with what was ahead of us, maybe he was saving that for later on.

We strode along the narrow path, where the gentle open fields on our right offered welcome visual relief from the dangerous cliffs only centimetres to our left; the frequent signage cautioning walkers to keep their distance. Olaf seemed oblivious to them, but I was confident he wouldn't go near the edge again.

We found our comfortable rhythm with Olaf reliably a few steps ahead, his walking poles gliding him along in steady, metronomic movements. I followed, grateful we couldn't possibly get lost again. All we had to do was stick to this eroded and etched path outlining England, ensure the North Sea was on our left, and inevitably we'd arrive in Filey in three days' time if everything went to plan.

A wooden-railed fence then herded us away from the edge, but the 'danger' signs continued to warn about the cliffs, as did the staggering number of sobering memorials on this stretch of the coast. This was clearly a place of great sadness and with it sat a palpable shroud of loss. It was difficult to reconcile on many levels but, given the life-affirming vistas all around, it amplified the sheer desperation and helplessness of those whose souls would remain here forever. Once again, we paused in the heaviness, then slowly moved on, past a Roman signal station, alongside a railway line which, until that moment, I hadn't managed to notice. I instinctively looked in both directions to work out how the track had magically appeared but became distracted by an intriguing circular object in the distance, over Olaf's right shoulder.

"What's that up there?" I asked, squinting to try and see.

"Not sure, but I guess we'll soon find out," Olaf replied. "Looks interesting."

"It does. Looks like some kind of public art, I think. I hope so, anyway."

About 200 metres on we could see exactly what it was – a large, cast-iron sculpture in the shape of a charm bracelet, standing about two metres tall. I loved it, touched it, walked around and through it. Dangling from its top were 10 three-dimensional 'charms', including a starfish, cat, mermaid and shovel, all linking to local folklore of the region's industrial past. I swatted each heavy charm and watched them swing with glee. Richard Farrington's artwork lifted our spirits and we continued on alongside the rail line in a happy silence.

Revelling in the peace and pace of nature, it dawned on me how calm the sea was, particularly given the North Sea's ferocious reputation. I'd expected that booming jet-engine crashing of waves to accompany us along the coast, the thunderous smashing noise so familiar from coastlines back home, but there was scarcely a peep from the water below. Well, that's how it was today anyway. It might deliver more in the days to come.

The security of the wooden fence disappeared and we moved along the cliff edge with greater caution once again. Ahead, I noticed a seaside village with a vast jetty and suggested we try and find some Devonshire tea. Olaf wasn't so keen, given the ground we still had to cover and the minimal distance we'd walked but he nodded and we silently slotted into our walking groove heading towards a jam and cream delight in Skinningrove.

The path dived from Cattersty Cliffs down steep steps onto

a stretch of beach where different muscles were needed for the very soft sand. We trudged through a gap in the old jetty, walked up the beachfront past some typical seaside cottages, and my legs turned to jelly.

"I know we haven't walked very far but I really need a break after that sandy slog," I said.

"Let's find us some scones," he said, as we walked down an empty cobbled street. "That might be easier said than done."

We didn't think we'd need to circumnavigate the town but when we ended up back where we'd started, we'd done exactly that. The only shop that was open was a small general store meaning our Devonshire tea plans were scuttled and the weight of disappointment, compounded with the thought of the kilometres still to cover, landed heavily in my thighs. We'd walked a mere 6.5 kilometres and the idea of walking another 21 seemed too much.

"I'll see what the general store has to offer," Olaf said, sensing my despondency. "Would you settle for an ice-cream if they've got one?"

"Well, it's not a scone, is it?" I said petulantly. "But yes, thank you, an ice-cream would be nice."

We ate Drumsticks on a beachfront seat and I had to admit, it was delicious, drank some water, threw on our packs and the day's long journey continued. We crossed a bridge towards the inevitable steep climb up steps to the cliff edge and my hopes for a less strenuous coastal walk were totally shattered. What had I been thinking, or not thinking, when we'd finished the moors section? Obviously, there were going to be ascents and descents with each inlet and cove, we'd have to scale up and down to continue along the Way, not to mention the energy-sapping sections of beach walking. It was definitely a case of wishful thinking gone wrong.

The cliff continued along Hummersea Scar for about 1.5 kilometres before the path turned away from the coast and skirted a small inland farm. Again, it felt like we were trespassers on private property and I even trod lightly as we walked right beside the stables and through a stile, which I declared a kissing gate because we hadn't seen one for a while. Olaf humoured my request and turned, bent and puckered his lips ready to receive mine. It felt like a heart-fluttering sneaky first kiss and I hoped the folk inside the close-by farmhouse either hadn't seen or didn't mind our public display of affection. Thankfully, no-one burst through the door, shaking their fists in the air, demanding we hurriedly leave. Of course, that wouldn't happen – this was a public path – but there was something romantically sneaky about that lovely moment.

Further along, the path returned to the precarious cliff edge where the visible rockface ahead had cleaved away dramatically leaving behind a stunning array of colours. The purple undergrowth either side of the path accentuated the vividly colourful stone and I had an *isn't nature incredible?* moment. For the next three kilometres we continued to see more of Mother Nature's fine work along the cliffs of England's east coast.

Light cloud cover persisted but the morning's pleasant breeze had disappeared, raising humidity levels and increasing my sweating. The air felt heavy and thick and the path ahead even had a haze across it, which appeared to get darker as we continued on. Then, a buzzing noise intensified and it was obvious what that dark haze was as we were enveloped by a gigantic swarm of flies. We flicked and swatted and didn't dare open our mouths in case we swallowed a pesky, sticky insect. It caught us totally off-guard as we hadn't even applied repellent and must've looked ridiculous from afar as we flailed around. I'd read midges and mosquitoes were active at certain times on this walk but flies hadn't rated a mention.

For about 200 metres our Australian salute continued, until at last, the buzzing pests thinned then disappeared. Emerging from the shroud, I took a deep breath, then expelled the lungful with great gusto, having held my breath throughout the 'great fly onslaught'. You'd think Aussies would be accustomed to having flies as company but this lot were insistent and dense and made us very uncomfortable. It was odd they were just in that one spot but I was grateful they preferred to stay put rather than follow us any further.

"What just happened?" Olaf asked, his hands still poised for stragglers.

"No idea. That was so out of place and so intense. I know I'm sweaty but didn't think I'd attract that many flies. Perhaps it's your smelly shirt they're chasing."

"Ha! Weird. I hope it doesn't happen again. That was hard work battling through."

"It was. Okay, from here on there's no flies on us."

"Exactly. Let's hope so, anyway." He smiled and we set off again.

As we regained our equilibrium and headed along the path again, I giggled to myself about the revenge I got on mosquitoes during chemotherapy. I figured if any mozzie was unlucky enough to bite me while I was having treatment, they didn't stand a chance against the toxic chemicals sloshing around in my veins. I could intravenously eliminate the blood-sucking buggers one at a time which was deserved payback for all those years of sleep-interrupting ear-drum flybys. It gave me a small sense of satisfaction at the time and made me smile even now.

Clifftop cottages greeted us at Boulby, along with contrasting grey chimneys of the town's potash mine, as the path became slippery with loose cut grass. We continued for nearly a kilometre before we reached the old coast road which was fenced off due to cliff erosion. It meant we had to detour inland and I was happy to get away from the treacherous edge.

"I'd love to come back in 30 or 40 years to see how much further inland the path would be then," said Olaf, "given all this erosion."

"When we're in our 80s. Let's hope our knees are up to it," I said, aware how lucky we were to even be there right then. We returned to our rhythm for almost three kilometres, scarcely speaking and feeling comfortable not to, until we could see our lunch destination.

The descent into the red-roofed, quintessential fishing village of Staithes was via a steep, narrow path which we inched down towards a narrow estuary. I scoffed aloud as we walked over the word SLOW painted on the path, unsure if it was a directive or an observation, but it was the only option heading into this port. My 'braking' muscles quivered, holding me on the gradient as I read a poem etched into the cliff face.

I was only three lines in when we came under siege again – not by flies this time - by deafening, giant, scavenging gulls dive-bombing us with intent. First, they bombarded Olaf and then turned on me for round two. Their ear-piercing squawks gained volume as they swooped then zoomed by. I whirled my walking pole above my head like a helicopter blade and Olaf joined in with his double offering, for protection. I'd never expected this to be a selling point for having two poles but I felt decidedly bereft with just one. I made a mental note to buy a companion for my singular, lonely pole ASAP.

After a few minutes of us whirling like maniacs, the monster gulls flew off, on their way to attack other unsuspecting walkers. Once more, it would've been an amusing sight watching us from afar, the birds well-practised in their choreographed assault and us flailing arms and poles in an unforeseen panic. The locals were probably used to it, though, as we weren't the first walkers this had happened to and definitely wouldn't be the last.

Having regained our breath and, to a lesser extent, our composure, we shuffled to the bottom of the path and crossed a bridge spanning the muddy expanse with beached boats stuck in the low tide of Staithes Beck. The path led into the main part of the village, its narrow, cobbled, winding streets heaving with tourists and activity. Cars could barely squeeze past one another and I winced and groaned as we saw several near misses in the space of a few minutes. There were noisy stand-offs and cars hastily reversing to break the traffic deadlock. Delivery trucks were abundant and skilled drivers somehow manoeuvred around without the loss of a side mirror or worse.

As the village bustled, I was ready for a proper lunch break and a chance to rest my tired legs and check my painful feet.

"Shall we skip the cheese today?" I suggested. "The Cod & Lobster is supposed to be good. We can grab a bowl of soup or something like that for a change." I was heading towards the waterfront before Olaf had time to respond.

"Right-o then. It's the Cod & Lobster by the looks of it," he said, as I sped off on my mission.

The cream-coloured building was striking with its blue shutters and prominent lettering and we found an outside table bathed in early afternoon sunshine. The sign offered pub food, cask ales and the odd lunch special and I was very happy to heartily partake in all three.

As I sat bayside, I felt that sensation you get when your tired body rests, a delightful release and joyous relaxation but it wasn't long before it was replaced by weariness knowing we were only at the day's halfway point. We still had another 13.5 kilometres to Sandsend. Olaf seemed flat and I went inside to order. In fact, he'd hardly moved since landing in his ample wicker chair. He'd always been strong throughout the whole cancer upheaval, maybe it was beginning to take a toll on his energy. He was a fixer in life, always keeping busy or planning ahead and was happiest when he had a task to complete or a problem to solve. He tackled my illness in that same framework – acknowledging the issue, formulating a plan, then working towards a solution – it was his modus operandi, his coping mechanism. But even he had a finite reserve of energy and it appeared he was flagging. When I returned with our two ciders, he had an unusual look on his face.

"I reckon my shirt needs a bloody good wash. It's really starting to stink," he said.

"Oh, you had me worried. If that's all, I'm sure we can find a laundromat in Whitby or perhaps you should soak it for a bit longer. You *have* given it a good hammering."

"Are we in Whitby tonight? I thought we finished in Sandsend."

"We *do* but apparently there's no accommodation there, so we'll get a taxi from there to Whitby and then back again in the morning."

"Right. Well, we've got to *get* to Sandsend first – somehow."

"Yeah. That still seems a long way to walk. Anyway, our vegetable soup will be here soon so let's enjoy that before we think about later. Cheers!"

"Cheers!" We clinked our glasses then slightly raised them to the sky.

"I think you're right about your shirt," I said, "I just got a waft and it's not good. Definitely needs attention tonight. No wonder those gulls were all over us – they must've thought you were some sort of stinky delicacy."

"What a morning: swamped by flies, swooped by gulls. I didn't see either of those things coming."

As we had our lunch and became more and more relaxed and my muscles got stiffer and stiffer, I secretly wanted to call it a day right there. It wasn't just to avoid any more encounters with gangs of critters, in truth, my legs felt a bit strange and I was a bit light-headed – not because of the cider – and then there were my feet. I'd see how I felt in a little while, after our lunch had settled and I'd had a chance to reassess. But I also didn't want to let Olaf down again with another incomplete day. I knew I was walking *my* Cleveland Way, but Olaf deserved to walk *his* too and if we finished today in Staithes, it would be a big chunk left unwalked. But for now, we sat in an easy silence overcome by inaction, tucking into our promised hearty grub.

We ummed and ahhed, then decided on another drink and I got the impression Olaf was happy to keep resting. I wondered if it was a good time to suggest finishing today's walk here but something told me it wasn't – not yet. The minutes ticked by and the afternoon's warmth brought with it feline-like sleepiness and drowsy yawns. Then, through heavy eyelids, I noticed a sign on the foreshore railing pointing up the steep incline of Church Street.

"I'm going to take a look at that art gallery up there. You stay here enjoying the sun," I said. "Well, actually, I'm not sure my legs can make it that far."

"It's only 200 metres, according to the sign."

"I know, but right now even that seems a long way, never mind 13.5ks to Sandsend," I groaned as I stood, leaving my comment to hang in the air. "I'll probably be about 20 minutes."

"No rush. I'll be here. Enjoy!"

Walking towards the gallery, I passed a narrow ginnel between two dwellings and, despite my reluctance to take more steps than I needed to, I walked back to have another look. It wasn't simply a gap between two buildings, it was Dog Loup, rumoured to be the narrowest street in England. At 45 centimetres wide, those skilled delivery drivers would struggle, even if they were on foot, and I easily resisted the temptation of a sideways shuffle along it, partly due to weariness but, mostly, thanks to claustrophobia.

The gallery was full of quirky, local art and crafts and I was immediately glad I'd popped in. I was instantly drawn to a black and white linocut print, *Staithes Rooftops*, and impulsively bought it on the spot. It was framed and small, but only after the sale did I wonder how it would safely travel for the remainder of the day, *should* we continue to Sandsend. I hadn't thought it through at all but I also didn't care – I loved it and was over the moon at my purchase. The gallery attendant wrapped the work in layers of extra-light bubble wrap which he assured would keep it safe and sound. I had a fleeting thought to ask for some extra to make those bubble wrap socks but then resisted the urge. It *did* remind me though, to check my feet when I got back to our table, 200 metres down the hill and, thankfully, downwind. Between Olaf's shirt and my socks, we could potentially clear the pub's clientele in an instant.

"What have you bought?" Olaf asked, when I returned after about 30 minutes.

"A gorgeous lino print but it's all wrapped up so you can't see it. I'm sure you'll like it," I said, as he shrugged and I gently tucked it into my pack.

By now, we'd been in Staithes well over an hour and a half and early afternoon had slid into mid-afternoon. It was time to tackle the elephant in the room – or at least on the foreshore.

"Shall I call a taxi to take us to Whitby?" I asked.

"I thought you'd never get around to asking. You've been thinking about that since we got here, haven't you?"

"Has it been that obvious?"

"Uh, just a bit."

"Well? What do you think? I'm spent, but if we keep missing bits of the walk, it's not fair on you." Even though I sensed Olaf was struggling today too.

"Hey, I'm fine and I'm more than happy to get a taxi from here." He rubbed his right knee in a clockwise motion without realising he was doing it.

"Thank goodness. But it's only because of the extra weight in my pack now. Obviously."

"Of course. Yeah, of course."

I headed inside to call a taxi and turned back to see Olaf now vigorously rubbing and wincing in pain. I know he would've walked the extra distance today if I'd been up to it but I'm sure he was relieved to rest his eroded joint for the rest of the day. My heart ached at how supportive he was and is, but my right hip ached more – a flare up in the sacroiliac joint – which I rubbed and poked to help ease the discomfort. Fifteen minutes later, we were on our way to Whitby, the landscape whizzing by as I sat in the back of the cab with a different perspective of farm life than on the prescribed trail.

Whitby is a large town, the largest we'd seen so far this walk. It felt odd to stop at traffic lights, give way at pedestrian crossings and speed along to our accommodation - Moor Edge Bed & Breakfast. Our host, Laura, was welcoming and informative and showed us to our ample upstairs room, with a large, comfortable bed, wide opening window and roomy shower, which I was very keen to use. As I got ready for this cleansing routine - grabbing fresh clothes, towel and toiletries – Olaf opened his backpack to empty it out.

"Holy hell!" he said. "Phwoar. Geez that stinks."

"What are you...? Oh god, that *does* stink," I agreed. "Is that your pack?"

"It's all this frigging cheese, that's what it is. It's -- phwoar. It's bad. Really, really bad."

"Oh god. It smells like disgusting feet and I should know. That's putrid. We'll have to chuck it out. It's done well, but it's clearly gone now. Is there much left?"

"Well, there's the Montgomery's we didn't eat today, I think. Oh, geez – that's ripe. Phwoar. And this chunk of Appleby's Cheshire. Thank goodness it's still wrapped but there's still a fair pong."

"Glad we didn't need it for lunch today then. Yuck. Do you think my future as a cheesemonger might've just crumbled? A bit like that cheddar? Pun intended."

"Now who's a goose? Anyway, you jump in the shower while I deal with this but I'm going to open that window to try to clear the room."

"Good idea. It needs it."

When I emerged from the shower, refreshed but still weary, Olaf was sitting on the bed smirking, his beloved blue shirt in hand ready to scrub. He sniffed it, inhaled deeply and gave a sigh, indicating a sweet fragrance. The shirt hadn't been the stinky culprit after all; it was clearly the pungent odour coming from the cheese we'd mistakenly assigned to his favourite garment. Perhaps tomorrow, without these malodourous foodstuffs on board, we'd be free from onslaughts by curious creatures.

Olaf showered and we headed to dinner at the Magpie Café which, according to *1001 Restaurants You Must Experience Before You Die*, is among the best fish and chips in all of England. Now, where have I read something similar recently? Its reputation must've spread as we joined the long queue snaking from its door along the waterfront, all of us eager to find out if the bold claim was justified.

We were seated within about 15 minutes and, for someone who wasn't usually a fan, I was eating a lot of fish and chips. Still, when in England, I guess it's best to do as the English do. It was a generous serve of cod, chips and Greek salad – perhaps not up to the standard of King George whiting back home in paradise – but we said cheers to Gunther anyway, just for fun. We chose to reserve our ranking until we'd sampled other 'best fish and chips' around the place but I thought it would rank highly. And now, there were only another 1,000 restaurants on the list to try!

Back at the aptly named Moor Edge, it wasn't long before we flopped into bed waiting to be taken into slumberland. As the evening light didn't quite turn to black, I lay wondering whether we'd failed today by quitting at Staithes and whether my guiding goal through treatment had faltered if we didn't do the whole walk. But mostly, I worried about my body holding up over the next few days. We'd walked just shy of 100 kilometres in six days with another 80 to do in the next three and I didn't know if I had the stamina for it. If the ache in my hip was anything to go by, it'd be a struggle. I hoped it wasn't more serious than the expected wear and tear, so I sent that 'other' thought off into the ether.

FEAR OF RECURRENCE

Fear of recurrence – it's a neat little phrase that encapsulates so many emotions and something anyone who's had a serious medical diagnosis knows well. It's the nagging voice in your head, the ever-present weight on your shoulder that serves to remind you of your situation, the 'sign' you keep seeing which says, "Hey, it might come back."

It's awful, it's real and it's completely normal and understandable. For a while, I didn't know it had a name but I certainly knew it existed.

Having harnessed all my energy to get through chemotherapy, when it finished, I almost felt a sense of abandonment. It was a case of what now, am I protected, how can I be sure the cancer won't return, how am I supposed to live my life? All the experts and support mechanisms I'd known for six months disappeared and I was on my own to deal with my fears. I felt like an adolescent who'd moved out of home, full of the joy of newfound freedom, yet right alongside sat the apprehension of facing life's unknowns without a safety net.

With every ache or pain, every bruise and sore spot, I was sure the cancer had returned. Even the universe was sending me signs, or so I thought, when I randomly opened the dictionary one day to page 1201 and saw the guide word at the top was 'metastasis'. I was convinced it was a sign – why else would I have opened to that page? And then there's all the media reports about new cancer treatments or someone losing their 'battle'. There were so many more of them - it had to be a sign. Plus, Doctor Google was never my friend, only confirming every possible fear I had. And the follow-up tests, scans and appointments where anxiety levels, or 'scanxiety', peaked at 11 – they were sure to confirm everything I'd feared.

So much for just 'keeping a positive attitude' which we're always told is a vital component along this path. I'd stayed relatively positive to this point but struggled to find my feet in this new world that was the rest of my life. My life view had permanently changed and, although I knew my fears were illogical, they were real, they existed and cast a shadow on everything. I needed to reprogram my thoughts.

Then I discovered the term 'fear of recurrence' – the name for everything I felt. It was a relief to have it so concisely explained, to know it was normal and be able to arm myself with ways to deal with it. I read extensively, now I knew what I was looking for and didn't feel isolated anymore. A few sessions with a personable psychologist helped enormously and together we created a box of tools to help manage my anxieties. Her analogy was to view my fear of recurrence (or FOR) like a tightrope walker viewing their challenge: respect the danger, acknowledge the fear, then step forward with courage. Yep, my logical brain could wrap around that but what about when anxiety manifested itself physically, like panic attacks?

"Focus on your breathing," she said. "You want to quieten your sympathetic nervous system and tap into the parasympathetic."

"Oh, you mean like yoga breathing?" I asked.

"Exactly like that. Take a deep breath, through your nose – do it now." I did as she instructed. "And inhale till your belly juts out. That's it. Now, exhale through your nose till your belly deflates. Simple. You'll probably only need to do it three or four times and you'll immediately feel less anxious."

"You're right, I feel calmer already. That's amazing. I should've remembered to do this all along."

"And whenever you have those 'other' thoughts, or you see a word on a page, surround it in a visualised bubble, send it off and say, 'that's just a thought'. It's gone, you've set it and yourself free."

"Okay. I can definitely make that work."

"Vicki, you didn't survive cancer to let it dominate your thoughts. Set those thoughts free and take a load off yourself."

Armed with this toolkit I felt better equipped to negotiate the maze of issues we 'first-time home-leavers' face in a world of discovery and uncertainty. I felt better able to transition to a self-reliant, non-fearful life and still find time to have some fun.

Day 7
SANDSEND TO ROBIN HOOD'S BAY
16 kilometres

Getting out of bed was a struggle as my body fought hard against the idea. Both hips now ached, my knees were sore but it was my feet that hurt the most. As I planted my right foot on the floor, the sharp dagger of plantar fasciitis thrust its way into my heel. Then, as I placed my left foot down, a loud cracking noise accompanied discomfort through the bridge and I sat straight back on the bed. It was not the welcome to the day I had expected or wanted and there were still the blisters to examine and treat. As I sat waiting for Olaf to wake up, I became teary with doubt about whether I'd be able to finish the walk. I'd come so far, fought so hard to get here and now it looked like I might not make it to the end.

"What's up?" Olaf asked, stirring himself awake.

"I'm just a bit down. My feet are stuffed and I'm not sure how much longer they'll last," I started to blubber.

"Hey! Come here." He moved to hug me. "Nobody ever said we're doing this for sheep stations. It's supposed to be fun, remember."

"I know," I sniffed loudly. "I know. It's just I've *needed* this walk for so long, if I don't finish it'll almost seem like a failure."

"You goose. You absolute goose. Just think about what you've done already and I'm not talking about how many ks we've walked. The last few months have been epic. Huge. And in case you missed it, you've been strong and amazing."

"Well, maybe I've been too strong and I can't take it anymore. Maybe pushing to keep working, pushing to get fit, pushing to ignore side effects, pushing, pushing, pushing, maybe it's all too much."

"Okay. Maybe. But what was the alternative? You *needed* that to get you through. Curling up in a ball wasn't an option, so this is where we've landed. Now, we'll sort your feet out and see how they go but so what if we change plans? Come on Wonder Woman, channel your inner warrior not your inner worrier. We'll be right."

"I'm just a bit sore and sorry for myself. But you're right, of course we can make our own rules, walk our own walk. I'm putting too much pressure on myself."

"Exactly. Now, let's get ready and see what the day brings."

I stood up gingerly to warm up my feet; the left foot now, thankfully, fine and the right one soon to follow. I blotted the blisters with a soothing cream and was cautiously pleased with how they looked – not as angry and pulsing – then wrapped them in their patchwork of bandaging. My big toes resembled something from an Egyptian tomb, the rest a hotch-potch of plaster. Organised for the day ahead, we headed downstairs to the light-filled breakfast room with several set tables and a huge buffet. We were the first to arrive and I was drawn to sit at a window-side table overlooking the bustling streetscape.

We loaded our bowls with cereal, fruit and yoghurt, poured ourselves coffee, just as another couple came in.

"Oh, hello, you two," the woman said, "I didn't think our paths would cross again."

"Morning," Olaf replied, looking quizzical at first. "Oh, yes. Hello to you too. Aren't you supposed to be a day ahead of us?"

It was Sheila, from day one in Helmsley. It was a surprise to see her and Andy again as I'd assumed they'd be way ahead by now.

"Yeah. How did that happen?" Andy asked, directing it to Sheila.

"I'm not sure. We must've taken two days to do what you did in one," she replied.

"Could've been between Saltburn and Sandsend – that was quite a long way," I offered, not admitting we'd stopped in Staithes.

"I think you're right. We walked Saltburn to Staithes, then Staithes to Whitby, and so today is a short day to Robin Hood's Bay," said Sheila. "To be honest, your nine days is a much better option than the 10 we're doing. Some days haven't been enough for me. Andy, on the other hand -"

"I'm very happy with a few shorter days," Andy said, smiling.

"Me too," I agreed. "We're doing Sandsend to Robin Hood's Bay today. Then Scarborough and onto Filey."

"Well, at this stage, I guess we're all heading to the same finish line," Andy added.

Two more couples came in and everyone busied themselves filling and refilling bowls, piling up plates and draining cups of coffee and tea. Laura took orders for cooked preferences and the room bubbled with a vibrant hum.

"I'm curious as to why you chose the Cleveland Way," I asked Sheila, sensing they were seasoned walkers.

"Oh, the diversity, the distance, the right level of challenge and it's been absolutely magic so far," Sheila said. "We come back to the UK every year to escape the Spanish summer; it gets so hot where we live. And we love walking, so we've combined the two and here we are."

"Same as us," I said. "Oh, not the bit about escaping the Spanish summer, the bit about the diversity and challenge and stuff." We laughed, as did another eavesdropping couple, my

Australian accent adding to the silliness of my comment. "How did you find the walk between Osmotherley and Clay Bank?" I tried to quickly cover my embarrassment.

"Pretty tough going, to be honest," said Sheila.

"Yeah, we've done quite a few walks in our time. Actually, more than quite a few," Andy added, "and that section was up there."

"Wasn't it just?!" the eavesdropping woman chimed in.

I shot Olaf a glance, hoping he'd keep our 'detour' a secret. Not that there was any shame in having taken that route, I just didn't want to share it with our fellow walkers.

"That last bit," Olaf said as I waited for the truth to come out, "how hard was it?" Unsure if it was a statement or question, I buttoned up and allowed others to decide.

"Super hard. Scrambling over the Wainstones was *not* my idea of fun," Sheila said. "At the end of a hard day - no fun at all."

It was enjoyable to share our stories and I was again buoyed to learn others also found parts of the walk challenging. It gave my confidence a real boost and was another validation that I was recovering well. Okay, maybe having pushed myself was a good thing after all. I thought it had been my reduced preparation that had made this walk tough at times, but obviously, parts of the Cleveland Way were hard for everyone. Unless you were the wiry couple who ran past us near Cringle Moor then on to Chop Gate – it didn't seem hard for them.

We finished breakfast and finalised preparations for the day's walk. I'd snaffled some pastries from the buffet for snacks and we still had the pears, but now we were cheese-less, we had to hope for a lunch opportunity on the way. We said our goodbyes and voiced our hopes that we'd run into each other again. I sensed, as couples we had very different walking paces, so chances were high we may not see them again. It was intriguing how multi-day walks seemed to pan out with no guarantees that paths would cross again. You had to enjoy the fellowship when you could.

The taxi dropped us at the Sandsend beachfront where we were supposed to finish yesterday if we hadn't called it a day in Staithes. It was overcast and dreary and a North Sea headwind meant our flimsy windproof jackets did nothing, even when fully zipped up. The misty sea-spray smeared my glasses and I needed some kind of automatic windscreen wiper rather than manually wiping them every few minutes. I tightly pulled down my out-of-place sunhat, trying to keep it on my head, as the brim offered a little peak which acted like a veranda over my specs.

It was our seventh day of walking and we'd been so lucky with the weather that it only struck me now how totally under-prepared we were with wet weather gear. I'd naïvely, or stupidly, assumed because it was summer the weather wouldn't be that bad.

"Well, it *is* summer," I had said when a local asked me back on day one if we had the proper kit. Now it made sense why it was met with laughter, a knowing shake of the head, and a muttering of something like, "Typical bloody Australians."

Still, we now had to make the best of it and with one foot in front of the other, we started the 16-kilometre walk towards Robin Hood's Bay. If the day had been fine and the tide out, we could've walked four kilometres on the beach to Whitby but I was pleased it wasn't even an option, given the toll the sand took on my legs at Skinningrove. Our only choice was to walk alongside the less picturesque A174. Over a bridge, we passed two hotels, and continued along the busy road before a greatly appreciated way-marker guided us inland away from the shoreline.

My yet-to-warm-up muscles went through their screaming phase and I struggled as the path climbed beside the Whitby Golf Club, down into a ravine, then underneath a footbridge built for golfers to use between strokes. As I stopped to catch my breath, we watched a group tee-off, walk across their purpose-built bridge, then move apart to address their next shots. They were all rugged up, clearly accustomed to the coast's icy greeting.

We left them to their round and skirted along the clifftop, our heads bowed against the elements, trying to get warm.

"Hey," I said, tentatively lifting my gaze, "that's Whitby Abbey up there. It's huge."

"It really is," Olaf said. "I'm not sure how we've only just spotted it, but it doesn't look too far away. It's impressive even from this distance."

"Sure is. And a bit foreboding or something." Its Gothic mysteriousness hovered around it, giving me a clear focal point to strive towards.

After passing multi-coloured beach huts, like those on the Mornington Peninsula in Victoria, we arrived in the town where we'd started our day, greeted by a statue of Captain Cook overlooking Whitby harbour. We continued under a whalebone arch honouring the town's past, then along the Khyber Pass Road which snaked steeply down to the busy quayside with its amusement arcades, fish restaurants and distinct white buildings with vibrant red roofs. The waterfront bustled with holidaymakers determined to enjoy their summer, despite the day's bleak weather.

"Poor buggers," Olaf said, "if this was your summer holiday and you had this miserable weather, you'd be pretty peed-off I reckon."

"God yes," I agreed. "Check out the ride operators, all rugged up, waiting for someone to hop on. I guess this is peak season, too."

"Yep, it would be. Hey – someone's jumping on that ride over there. All is not lost. Maybe that'll get some others going. A bit like being the first up to dance."

"I hope so for their sake." I wiped my glasses yet again, the misty drizzle now having total disregard for my ingenious makeshift brim.

We crossed a swing bridge over the River Esk and walked into the narrow old part of town, down quaint cobbled streets leading to the market square. After twists and turns through medieval streets lined with tiny cottages, we arrived at the base of the silhouetted ruin and 199 steps to St Mary's Church and Whitby Abbey. I was again amazed at the ground we'd covered even if I was slow. What felt like, only moments before, had been a way-off-in-the-distance destination, we were now nearing a close-up look at the striking abbey.

The steps were wide and gentle and a very easy climb. I didn't bother counting - others were doing that aloud – and I was confident if there *weren't* 199, someone probably would've noticed by now. We arrived at the top where the giant former monastery's shadow was brooding; its eerie presence an obvious inspiration for Bram Stoker's novel, *Dracula*, penned after he'd stayed here in 1890. Or perhaps it was the ghostly presence of St Hild, the stern Saxon princess who once ruled the abbey, disapproving of loud tourists and their excesses, given her strict monastic commitment to piety and chasteness.

The drizzle turned to rain, which added to the heavy atmosphere. A quick and obvious decision was made to head inside the modern National Trust shop, along with throngs of tourists clearly thinking the same thing. I visited its toilet facilities – a luxury on a walk – then browsed the usual suspects of souvenirs until the rain eased. Back outside and following the signs once more, we circumnavigated the manicured perimeter before heading along the cliff's edge again towards our destination. A way-marker authoritatively signalled 10.5 kilometres to go and I was deflated to realise we hadn't even reached today's halfway point. A slight and persistent drizzle continued and my sunhat stayed firmly rammed on my head with mixed success at shielding my glasses. The high humidity and a hot flush adding to the visual impairment.

"I can't see a damn thing," I said. "My glasses keep fogging up and I'm as hot as hell."

"Well, if it gets too bad," Olaf chuckled, "you can use your walking pole like a cane. I'll let you know if you get too close to the edge."

"You can't say that! And besides, it's not funny and not helpful. Anyway, I'll be okay in a few minutes, I hope."

"Good. But I'll still let you know if you get too close."

"How? You're always five steps ahead of me." And as if proving my point, he'd already walked off with a sense of determination.

I gulped water as we walked and was soon on the other side of the flush. The drizzle had stopped, allowing me to take off my hat and the cooling effect was immediate. I caught up to Olaf and we slotted back into our rhythm, leaving Whitby Abbey in our wake; its imposing silhouette like an ominous shadow hovering behind us. I turned around for one final glimpse and an intense shiver shook me. It may have been the after effect of the hot flush but it was unnerving, so I picked up my pace to catch up to Olaf, now quite a way ahead. He must've sensed I'd dropped back and was waiting for me to catch up.

Just over a kilometre on, the track led into a busy caravan park and I spotted a sign pointing to a kiosk. Now I fancied an ice-cream and so did Olaf.

"Hello, you two," said a woman's voice as we approached the kiosk door.

"Oh, hi," I replied. It was Sheila. "I thought you'd be hunkered down in Robin Hood's Bay by now, especially with this drizzle."

"We're using today as a bit of a rest day, so we're having lunch here and will take our time the rest of the way."

"You'll still beat us there. Your cruising speed is way faster than us even when we're flat chat. I'm so slow and do a lot of huffing and puffing. Olaf's always waiting for me."

"Oh, we huff and puff too," said Andy, finishing a mouthful of bacon and egg roll. "Well, *I* do anyway. Besides, it's not a race, is it? Geez, I hope it isn't, otherwise we've totally blown our chances today."

Olaf chatted further as I bought the ice-creams, which we decided to eat as we continued to walk.

"I'm sure you'll pass us soon," I said, bidding them farewell.

"If not, we might see you in Robin Hood's Bay," said Sheila.

"Hopefully," Olaf muffled through a mouthful of Cornetto, "bye - for now."

With eight kilometres left, we were now halfway through the day and I found a spring in my step. I hadn't given my feet a thought which meant the strapping and wrapping must've been working for the moment. I attributed my new-found pep to the sugar hit from the ice-cream but I think it came from the warmth and camaraderie developing with Sheila and Andy. It felt like there was a connection and commonality in our senses of humour and joy of walking but I also got a sense they wanted to keep a distance and not get too close. It was subtle but it was there and I took it on board. Still, I hoped we *would* see them later that day but that was unknown and all part of the fun.

Emerging from the caravan park, the path returned to the cliff's edge and I was excited to see a kissing gate ahead. Olaf arrived there first, went through, puckered up across the railings and I obliged with a gentle peck. To my delight, he had a tiny speckle of chocolate on his lower lip, so I went back for a second peck to retrieve it before passing through. It was only a small thing but that split-second moment made everything worth it.

Another kilometre on we passed a private home which was once the Whitby Fog Signal Station. Its occupants, I'm sure, were pleased its horn was no longer used. According to our guidebook, it would belt out four blasts every 90 seconds back in the day when conditions were foggy, which must've been both deafening and maddening for anyone nearby. We kept on alongside a perimeter wall surrounding an imposing lighthouse, then gently climbed to a higher path along the Widdy Head clifftop. Although we'd struck it when it was calm, the precariousness of the North Sea was evident and had clearly been the bane and, often ruination, of tens of thousands of vessels over time. I felt silly for whingeing about my fogged-up glasses earlier. Those seamen really couldn't see a damn thing and their battles in the thickest of mists had been real and often deadly.

"Look at those birds," I said, snapping back to the present.

"They're almost defying gravity. And they are noisy," yelled Olaf.

"How are their nests clinging to that ledge?"

"No idea but it's amazing engineering. And with these guys around, I don't reckon you'd need to use the foghorn - they're so loud."

"Nature's own warning device."

"Hey?"

"Never mind."

We hastily passed the decibel-busting flock and slotted into single file, thankful the mist and drizzle of the day was only an occasional and short-lived nuisance.

Steep and slippery steps took us down into a wooded valley which was slow going, with every foot placement crucial to avoid slipping or tweaking a joint. Across a stream and then, of course, another set of steps to climb to cross a ravine, then up to the clifftop. Another kilometre along, a way-marker showed the Coast to Coast Walk had joined us again for its final five kilometres into Robin Hood's Bay. What a thrill and relief it must be for those walkers to reach the 'other side' of England. But, I thought, that thrill would be short-lived with another steep descent into a gully, across two footbridges, then back up the obligatory climb to the top. My legs now screamed, my face blared red and buckets of sweat poured from everywhere, so I politely suggested we take an urgent break.

I grabbed our water bottles from Olaf's pack and plonked down on a bum-shaped mound, tailormade for the occasion.

"Almost there," a man said, coming up behind us. It turned out to be Andy offering this hackneyed walkers' phrase; Sheila was right behind.

"It's only because I can see it that I believe you," I said, pointing to the distant headland. They'd predictably caught up, looking relaxed, fresh and sprightly as their 'light' day clearly agreed with them. They continued walking and were soon well ahead of us.

It was now mid-afternoon with a little over two kilometres left and, although it felt so near, it also felt miles away. Even after this brief rest stop, my hips didn't want to restart and, after a few steps back on the path, I noticed Olaf limping. And then the misty drizzle returned and I wanted to be in Robin Hood's Bay already – dry and resting. Instead, I jammed down my hat, ignored my rain-speckled, fogged-up glasses and put one foot in front of the other on the way to the nearing village. After 15 minutes or so, we were on its outskirts, overlooking a network of tangled streets which sharply descended towards the hidden fishing bay of this once-infamous smuggling port.

Luckily for my tired thighs and overused braking muscles, our B&B – The Villa - was at the top of the town. I'd had enough steep descents for one day so was ecstatic to find we didn't have to do another one – just yet. Dripping wet, we met our host, Helen, who was very direct with her house rules, starting with exactly where to place wet shoes, walking poles and a request to walk with a light footfall. I half-expected her to say, 'There'll be no laughter allowed either.' She told us she liked her guests to be back from dinner by 9pm – okay? Right.

She led us upstairs to our room and delivered more instructions there; it wouldn't have been out of place for her to say, 'At ease' as she left. Olaf closed the door and we stood silent for a second before bursting into subdued giggles, scared she may still be lingering outside, so we quietly jiggled and shook until we sensed the coast was clear. I finally offloaded my damp clothes and indulged in a warm shower, while Olaf went about his usual laundry routine.

The rain was now heavy and the extremely steep descent to the village centre for dinner felt precarious as we slowly passed rows of cottages with their flowering pots and colourful doorways.

"How's your knee with this?" I asked, halfway down the hill.

"Sore as usual and this slippery road doesn't help. You be careful, I don't want you taking a tumble - again. Not now!" he said.

"Don't worry. I'm going slower than my usual tortoise pace here. But I was just thinking it'll be interesting on the way home; we might have to leave by 8:00 to make sure we're home by 9:00. Otherwise, who knows what might happen."

"Mmmmm. Well, let's not find out. I really need a comfy bed tonight. But she might have our -"

A high-pitched scream stopped us immediately as a very large, 20-something woman fell awkwardly only 10 metres in front of us. She yelled in pain as she sprawled motionless across the footpath, unable to right herself and obviously in a lot of discomfort. We moved quickly to help but, even in her agony, she tried to send us away, pleading to be left alone. I can only assume it was shock or embarrassment at the source of her desire but we weren't going to simply leave her.

"Are you sure you're okay?" Olaf asked.

"I'm fine, thank you," she said, grimacing. "You just keep going."

"Are you sure?" Olaf checked. She nodded and we slowly moved away.

But Olaf hovered, unconvinced about her welfare, as I headed to a shop down the street to try to get some help. But she *did* need help and was on the verge of a panic attack when Olaf returned to her side. He reassured her, guided her through some breathing and offered her a sip of water. As I walked back from the closed shop, I had a sense of déjà vu; I was sure I'd seen a similar scene somewhere before.

A group of four people, who'd been quite a way behind us, arrived and the much calmer woman was now agreeable to some help. Olaf positioned everyone for the lift and together they moved her to a seat out of the rain. Her face showed that she was a lot more comfortable and a quick assessment revealed she wasn't badly hurt. After multiple statements of gratitude, she insisted on calling her sister who, she assured us, would arrive shortly. She wanted us to keep going, leave her alone and she waved us on our way but we stayed nearby until assistance arrived.

Waiting there, I remembered where I'd seen this scene before. It was a trip to the Flinders Ranges Olaf and I had taken soon after we'd met. It was our first challenging walk, a 21-kilometre loop, including the 1,189-metre climb up St Mary Peak and I was excited we were doing this together. So, on a cold, clear July morning, we set off with enthusiasm and, for me, naivety at what lay ahead.

After a solid couple of hours climbing and scrambling over large, slippery boulders, teetering along an escarpment edge and becoming fatigued, we reached the iconic peak where Olaf produced a bottle of sparkling wine to celebrate. But the fierce windchill and signs of waning afternoon light had us on the move within minutes as the descent had to be slow and careful.

Having negotiated the first tricky part of the downward trek, we encountered a man, aged around 70, whimpering and slumped across the narrow path.

"You okay, mate?" Olaf asked, bending down to check his pulse.

"No. I'm a bit crook," he whispered. "I can't move. I'm cramping."

We sat with him and discovered he'd only drunk half a litre of water for the entire climb and, although it was a cold, winter's day, he'd seriously underestimated his hydration needs. Olaf handed the man one of his own full bottles and demanded he drink the lot.

"I'll be okay. The cramp will be gone soon, you keep going," the man said, waving us on.

"Nah, nah, nah, we're not going anywhere. You *need* to drink it and eat some of this," Olaf insisted, offering him some chocolate.

As he sipped the water and slowly ate the chocolate, my mind went into catastrophe overdrive at the lack of phone signal and we waited for him to show signs of improvement. But what if he didn't improve - how would we get him down? Would we have to carry him or just leave him to his own devices? And how much light did we have left in the day before temperatures really dived?

Just as my panic was about to boil over, the man stood up and said he was fine and, again, wanted us to be on our way. Thank goodness. He'd be on his way soon. So, I grabbed my pack, ready for the two of us to continue the significant remainder of the circuit but Olaf wasn't having any of it. After a bit of convincing, we accompanied the man the 10 kilometres back to the car park, with Olaf carrying all his gear, along with ours, and keeping him engaged throughout. Having arrived back at our cars under a jet-black sky, punctuated by millions of jewel-like stars, with the temperature rapidly headed downwards, Olaf went to shake the man's hand and wish him well but he'd already taken his belongings and walked off towards his vehicle – without a single word. Not a thank you, not an acknowledgement at having put all our lives at risk. Not one single word.

The fallen woman's sister arrived, releasing us to continue our search for a dinner venue but I couldn't help but wonder why she and the man in the Flinders, all those years ago, had refused help when they clearly needed it. And I'd done the same thing myself only weeks before at Minyon Falls - was it pride or was it shock? I figured it was probably both and resolved to be more like Olaf in those situations, who wouldn't accept their initial refusals. We'd had a few 'moments' in our various adventures, luckily with positive outcomes and here in Robin Hood's Bay there was yet another tale to add. That idea, sown two nights ago in Saltburn, was starting to bed itself in.

Still a little shaken, we walked further down the precarious street where a small, inviting pub beckoned and we decided The Laurel Inn was for us. Olaf ducked under the low doorway as we entered the busy, dark, wood-panelled hub and scanned the room for a spare table.

"Well, hello you two!" Sheila called out from across the room.

"Sheila, Andy, hi!" I said, "long time, no see."

"Grab a seat, I'll get some drinks," said Andy, already out of his seat. They'd clearly been there a little while, tell-tale empty lager glasses and a crisp packet the giveaway. I sat down as Olaf joined Andy on the way to the bar.

"I'm glad we've bumped into you again," I said, "but you never know if that's going to happen, do you?"

"No, that's so true. It's good to see you too. How did you find today? Obviously, ours was pretty easy but how are you going?"

"We're going okay. I had my moments today but not too bad. My feet aren't in great shape and I've got some sore spots, but otherwise fine. It's Olaf's knee I'm worried about. It's being replaced two weeks after we get home and I think it's giving him grief. Not that he'd let on."

"Oh boy!" She paused. "If you don't mind me saying, it looks like you've had your challenges recently too."

Her comment took me aback for a moment, probably

only a split second. I'd hoped my hair was at that point where it might've been considered a brave and contemporary choice. Clearly not.

"Yes. I finished chemo a couple of months ago now, thank goodness. Honestly, focusing on this walk really got me through."

"Oh boy. I thought it must've been chemo or the like. I *love* your hair, by the way."

"Thank you." I ruffled it, still amazed at the growth over this week.

"It looks great. Such a gorgeous colour."

"Oh, I absolutely *love* the colour. I'm feeling all Dame Judi Dench with it." I figured I'd be stretching it now with the Annie Lennox comparison but was more than happy with my newly assigned likeness. "I'd love it to stay like this but it won't. I'm naturally dark, so this is a surprise and lots of fun."

"Well, between the two of you, it's a feat to even be here. You're quite the inspiration. You certainly put us to shame."

"Hardly. We really are tortoises and I'm forever having tantrums about one thing or another. Anyway, it's just good to be here. I hope we can get through the next two days and finish this walk."

The men arrived with the drinks, Olaf with crisps tucked under his arm, and we raised and clinked our glasses to a chorus of *Cheers!*

The conversation and bonhomie continued for another hour or so as we ate dinner and exchanged familiar stories. But I was still processing Sheila's earlier comment that she thought I'd been through chemo or the like and wondered why it surprised me so much. Yes, I was feeling good about my hair growth – maybe a bit unrealistically - but more importantly, I felt totally comfortable sharing my story, even if it was only a snippet of a bigger tale to tell.

Serendipitously, Andy and Sheila were also staying at The Villa and together, we headed back up the steep road to our

B&B. Thankfully, the rain had abated and, although the streets were still slippery, it was so much easier and we arrived back at around 8:45pm - we'd made curfew! Their room was the floor above ours, so we said goodnight and they continued up the staircase. I could barely keep my eyes open and slid under the purple, velvet bedspread ready for sleep. Tomorrow was another long day with Scarborough 23.5 kilometres away, so a good rest and plenty of bandaging were needed if we were to make it. Olaf joined me under the cover and we naturally locked into our 'spoons' position.

"Sweet ones, beautiful," he said as I drifted off to sleep.

YOU'RE BEAUTIFUL

For most of my adult life I've been on the beauty 'hamster wheel' of plucking, shaving, waxing, cutting and colouring hair, complying with society's preconceived idea of beauty. But truth be known, I've never been terribly diligent with it, just lucky to be at the lower end of the hirsuteness scale and able to get away with the odd lapse here and there. But being a natural brunette, who chose to be strawberry blonde, a regular hairdresser visit was a time-consuming and costly necessity. I'd emerge from the salon reset and ready to tackle the world but I would never have said I felt beautiful.

In fact, beautiful is *not* how I'd describe myself. It never has been and never will be and I'm at ease and comfortable with that. From an early age, it becomes clear where we sit on the beauty spectrum and I've always felt mid-range on the human scale of attractiveness - not pretty, not ugly, somewhere smack bang in the middle. We middle-of-the-roaders know it's a crowded place and I've enjoyed hanging out with that particular crowd. Of course, we're told beauty is skin-deep and in the eye of the beholder, but everybody has a rough idea of how they scrub up, which then impacts on self-esteem and self-worth regardless of our inner 'beauty'.

And beautiful is not a word others would ascribe to me

either, apart from Olaf who himself is beautiful in every sense (I'm showing my bias here, obviously) but words like cute, quirky, cheeky, feisty, even cherubic have been much more common. So, when my body was at its most ravaged, after months of chemotherapy, and without a single hair follicle anywhere to be found, it came as an enormous shock to be told I was beautiful. And not just once, it happened repeatedly. Initially, I thought it was out of pity or concern but it kept happening on social media and more awkwardly face-to-face. At first, I was overwhelmed and disbelieving, not used to being described this way and then I became intrigued. Maybe it was like those 'good-shaped head' comments where people didn't know how to react or what to say or maybe they were looking through 'empathy goggles' with kinder filters attached. Words like classy, elegant, glowing and sparkling were now being used but the runaway, chart-topping descriptor was beautiful.

I learned it's a phenomenon known as 'chemo-glow', a rare occurrence where paradoxically your skin looks taut and radiant and you appear the picture of health, even if you don't feel it. So ironically, for the first time in my life I was beautiful. After all those years of primping and preening, it was only when I was completely hairless that I was seen as beautiful. Of course, it provided a timely confidence boost, as I still faced more treatment, but it also made me ask why I'd stayed on that hamster wheel for so long and question what I'd do when my hair grew back. I loved the idea of being liberated from that ongoing cycle, embracing the gifts I'd been born with but I'd face that hamster when the time came.

Day 8
ROBIN HOOD'S BAY TO SCARBOROUGH
23.5 kilometres

Breakfast was akin to a military-style operation with Helen on patrol. Her insistence on who sat where, what food to have in which order and how long it should take, was the antithesis to a relaxing start to the day. Olaf and I were first in the breakfast room and had just finished receiving our instructions when Andy and Sheila came in and were promptly delivered the same drill. The look on Sheila's face was priceless or perhaps it was shock but she was clearly not expecting our host's manner. We dared not to look at each other until Helen had left the room. As soon as she was gone, we broke about laughing.

"That's equal to anything I experienced in the army," Andy said. "Is anyone brave enough to have toast *before* their cereal or yoghurt?"

"No!" The three of us said.

Obeying orders, I got some fruit and yoghurt, while the others filled their bowls and plates as well. Then, what seemed like only minutes later, there were footsteps in the hallway.

"Everyone ready?" Andy smirked.

"Y'alright?" asked Helen, entering the room. "All done?"

And she whisked away my not-quite-empty bowl as I was still chewing. I nodded.

With breakfast over, we returned to our room and readied ourselves to tackle the penultimate day. Not only was it 23.5 kilometres – one of the longer sections of the walk – but the terrain was undulating, diving into wooded valleys then climbing back up to cliff tops. I desperately hoped my body was up to it. We took our luggage downstairs, ready for the Sherpa van, then adjusted our walking poles and put on our laden packs. Except my pack wouldn't cooperate. The strap across my chest wouldn't clip in and I jiggled it around to try to release it from wherever it was caught.

"Having trouble there, love?" Helen asked, heading towards the breakfast room.

"Yeah, it won't do up across here for some reason," I replied.

"Ah, yes. I've got big boobs too. Sometimes I wish I could just chop 'em off."

Her remark hung in the air as she kept walking. Olaf's eyes went big and he held his breath, unsure of how I'd react. Was it too insensitive, too hurtful and too soon after my mastectomy? But none of those applied, instead I felt a weird sense of comfort in her assessment of my body, the gel-filled bra was fulfilling its purpose and she hadn't even considered my boobs were not my own. And then I suddenly thought, *be careful what you wish for, Helen*. The buckle then clicked into place and we were ready to go.

We farewelled Andy and Sheila, who recalcitrantly lingered over breakfast, confident our paths would cross during the day as they were sure to overtake us at some point. And so, we headed off down the steep road we'd tackled the day before, this time without incident. With all the drama of the woman's fall yesterday and an enjoyable dinner at the pub later, I'd momentarily forgotten about my body's weariness, blistered feet, aching hips and clicking left knee. However, they were all now vying for attention. The nerve damage in my feet was, for the most part, horrible but perhaps the lack of sensation today was a blessing. Everything *really* hurt and the 'screaming and rattling' was going to take some getting through.

We carefully ventured towards the waterfront, stopping at a small and inviting grocery shop to stock up with fruit and bread rolls, given we weren't having a cheese-fest anymore, which saddened my inner rodent. It felt like a valued travelling companion had parted ways and we'd need to fill the void. Today, large chunks of ham and some juicy tomatoes would attempt to take its place.

As we walked through Robin Hood's Bay with its small cottages clinging to the rocks, its dark, underworld notoriety of yesteryear seemed in sync with the day's weather. Yesterday's rain had disappeared, but it was overcast, humid and not a breath of wind. It was a day with the potential to easily sap energy, so I needed to stay hydrated, given the amount of sweat I would lose, with a lot of drink stops along the way.

Relieved to have made it to the bottom of the steep-pitched road, I knew it wouldn't be long until there'd be its counterbalancing climb. We trundled past the Smugglers Bistro, down a lane to Flagstaff Cottage, climbed a set of narrow stone steps, then up again on a wooden stairway, until we arrived on the clifftop.

"My legs are like jelly," I said, puffing.

"Your face is bright red too," Olaf said.

"And I can't even say it's a hot flush. I'm just hot after that climb."

"Do you want to stop for a bit? Have some water."

"Nah, not yet. We've hardly even started. Let's get to Ravenscar and have a coffee and scone. So, lead on, Macduff." I double-tapped his bum.

"Okey-dokey. Ravenscar it is."

It took about two kilometres for me to settle into a rhythm as we walked side by side along a wide, fenced path; it was a nice change to the usual narrow walkways which forced us into single file. Open pastureland to our right housed contented-looking cows and the sheer, subsiding coast to our left was covered in overgrown native grass along with a smattering of purple and white flowers. As we clung to the eastern edge of England, if there had been any roses I would've smelt them, but I stopped anyway to take it all in. Patches of blue sky had burst through the grey and Mother Nature momentarily showed off. The North Sea was still calm and the coastland ahead displayed every shade of green, even though it was the middle of summer; something we could hardly imagine back home. Behind us, Robin Hood's Bay nestled into its coastal hideaway, wispy wildflowers swayed, thanks to a much-appreciated zephyr breeze, and I took a good glug of water.

"Hello, you two," Sheila said approaching us from behind.

"Oh, hi! Are you stalking us?" I joked. They hadn't taken long to catch up.

"I guess we are in a way," she added. "We *do* seem to be bumping into you an awful lot." She gestured with quote marks to suggest 'bumping into' was a stretch.

"I told you, we were tortoises but I didn't think you'd be 'haring' past us just yet."

"We're pushing on to have a break in Ravenscar. There's tearooms there apparently."

"Same as us. That's our planned break stop."

"We'll probably see you there, then." They were already walking off.

"Yeah, maybe." I said but doubted it.

Within minutes they were a pink and red dot in the distance and I deduced their walking pace must be at least double ours and then they were nowhere to be seen, not even dots on the horizon. We ambled along through a hand-cut tunnel of overgrown, coarse bracken towards Boggle Hole. There were more steep, slippery steps to climb down leading into a wooded ravine and I slowed down even more as I was determined not to fall. Each step was deliberate and steady and I tucked my pole under my armpit to grip the wooden handrail with both hands. When we reached the dark and damp ravine floor, I breathed out as I'd held my breath most of the way down. It took a few moments to return to normal. Then we crossed a footbridge and passed a youth hostel, to find a way-marker that promised Ravenscar was four kilometres away. I could push on that distance, with the alluring prize of Devonshire tea promised when we got there. Again, I wondered where my head was at, presuming this coastal section would be easier than the moorland. What on earth had I been I thinking?

Sensing my slight hesitation and knowing there was a steep climb imminent, Olaf led us through a thicket which opened onto a small, rocky beach and we decided to have another drink break and share a banana. It was bliss. We sat for about 10 minutes overlooking the glass-like water in what felt like our own tailormade cove. I wanted to remember that moment forever, not just because it was nice to be off my feet, but because it was as though we were the only two people on the planet. I closed my eyes and imprinted a deliberate mental snapshot to 'come back here' whenever I needed to in future. But we needed to keep walking with Scarborough still 20 kilometres away – a deflating thought for my weary body, given we'd only walked a few kms.

We left the tranquillity and climbed what seemed like 1,000 steps back up to the clifftop. Humidity levels felt like 100%, which meant foggy glasses, a sweaty face and a slightly fraying temperament. That moment of serenity and calm back on the beach had dissipated too soon and we faced yet another steep descent back down to sea level. I couldn't help but wonder whose idea it was to do this silly walk. I really wanted to crack it and say I'd had enough, but that wasn't what had got me through all those months. I hadn't stayed focused on doing this walk to have a childish tantrum and call it quits now. I had to get over myself and keep pushing on, even though my tired body was rallying against that prospect.

We crossed another footbridge and then a steep climb led to a road and then to some flat terrain – not before time. The level ground provided welcome respite and gave me a chance to again look back along the coastline at Robin Hood's Bay playing hide and seek in the cliff face. From this angle, you could see why it had been chosen as the perfect smugglers' haven. I turned back onto the path where there were loud squawking noises somewhere ahead, which got louder and louder as we continued.

"That almost sounds like peacocks," I said, recalling a childhood memory of the birds in Whyalla, "but what would peacocks be doing around here?"

We rounded a bend and Olaf said, "Well, there you are – it is peacocks. And *that's* what they're doing here."

"Wow! I didn't expect that."

"No. Wouldn't have thought Yorkshire was the ideal place for a peacock farm but there you go. Look at that one showing off. They can't help themselves, can they?"

"All those gorgeous feathers. It reminds me a bit of what we saw at *Moulin Rouge*."

"That's not what I remember about *Moulin Rouge*. Must've been focusing on other things." Olaf gave a cheeky grin and I gave him a playful whack. We continued past this strange, out of place muster, feeling as though we'd had some misplaced encounter.

Back along the cliff's edge and past a wartime bunker, until 1.5 kilometres further on, the Way turned inland across a field, then veered right up a wide, steep path. My head was down and tail determinedly up, to get to Ravenscar ASAP and it felt like Olaf was pulling me along in his wind-resistant wake, my legs feeling almost separate to my body. The ground underfoot then became pockmarked with jagged chunks of brick and I really had to concentrate to avoid rolling my ankle. But with my focus now downwards, it wasn't my ankle of concern, I noticed my left knee had swollen as I'd trudged through my increasing fatigue. I poked its squishy form and cursed that previous fall near Byron Bay which I thought was well behind me. As the path surface improved, I looked up and, to my relief, saw we were only 100 metres from the Ravenscar visitor centre where I was happy to stop for our break.

I sat at an outside table ready to fully assess my knee and took a deep, wincing breath in but before I could exhale, a thick swarm of flies had joined me, clearly attracted to my sweaty presence and, in a repeat performance of days before, sent my arms into a flapping frenzy. I gathered up my gear before Olaf sat down and we escaped inside. I exhaled, safe in the knowledge I wouldn't swallow a buzzing beast, then found there was no airflow in the place. Sweat dripped off my crimson face and I removed as many clothes as I decently could to quickly cool down and wondered why there were no ceiling fans in the UK and why there was a national obsession to not let a breath of air into any room. Logically, I knew it was the 'keep warm' mind-set intrinsic to most Brits but it was the complete opposite to my antipodean 'stay cool' thinking. My recently acquired hot flushes didn't help that either, I suppose.

After five minutes, my thermostat had returned to normal and I was keen to tuck in to that Devonshire tea before fully checking out all my ailments. I hobbled to the counter ready to order with my purse poised to get it happening quickly but the attendant simply pointed me to a hot-water urn and instant coffee sachets at the end of the bench. Oh, and there were pre-packaged pastries too, should I wish to 'splash out'.

No coffee and no scone – *no way!* I returned emptyhanded to our table and sat opposite Olaf.

"I really *needed* that scone, that jam and that cream," I said.

"They've only got pastries which are probably a week old and instant frigging coffee. NOT HAPPY, JAN!"

I think he'd worked that out.

After a considered pause, Olaf said, "It could be a lot worse, you know."

"Oh, yeah. How?"

"You really need me to point that out?" He took off towards the counter. "I'm getting you a pastry and me a Cornetto. Now, get a grip."

As he got our food, I felt stupid at my over-reaction and wondered why I was worrying about the small stuff today rather than taking it in my stride. Minor setbacks and a few major ones, over the preceding 12 months were far more 'tantrum-worthy' than missing out on Devonshire tea. But when you're tired, little things become big and I was unsure about my body. Still, it was ridiculous to get uptight with the visitor centre and with Olaf. It was hardly their fault I'd pushed myself to walk the last 120 kilometres with less-than-ideal preparation. So, when Olaf returned with a Danish in one hand and an ice-cream in the other, I apologised for being a brat. I took a bite and it was delicious and squeezed Olaf's free hand as another sign that I was sorry. He squeezed back and, from his chocolate-flecked lips, mouthed, *I love you*. It set me off and, once again, I became teary but, even through the blurriness, saw two familiar figures entering the shop. I wiped my eyes with the back of my hand.

"Hello, you two!" I said, before Sheila got in first. "How the heck did we beat you here? I thought you'd be long gone."

Sheila was surprised too.

"Oh, hello you two, yourselves. I didn't expect to see you either. We're a bit behind because we spent time on the beach near Boggle Hole; longer than we'd planned, actually. It was so lovely we didn't want to leave." They took off their packs and sat with us.

"We stopped there too," I added. "I thought we were all

alone but you must've been there already. Strange we didn't see you."

"We *did* tuck ourselves into an alcove out of sight. It was so lovely. I guess we had to be there at the same time as you. And what about that last bit just here – that was tougher going than I expected."

"I know! I thought it was just me, so I'm glad you found it tough too. That makes me feel a lot better."

"I'd kill for a coffee," Andy said glancing towards the counter.

"I hope you like instant," Olaf said, "because that's all they've got."

"You're kidding?" He wasn't happy either. "Well, that's a bugger. We were going to stop at the tearooms further on but decided on here instead and now it's too hard to get moving again. I'll just have a cold drink instead, I guess."

Sheila went and ordered and, when she returned, the conversation for the next quarter of an hour focused on the task ahead – the remaining 17 kilometres to Scarborough. The thought made me shudder.

"I'm not sure I can do it," I said, certain I was letting Olaf down again.

"Right. Not feeling up to it?" Olaf asked, reaching for the guidebook.

"I'm already spent and another 17 kilometres just seems impossible. Besides, have a look at this knee. And I think there's some bleeding in my sock. Maybe you three could walk together and I'll meet you later on. Or is piking out being pathetic?"

It'd be another day we'd fallen short of the target.

"It's hardly pathetic," Sheila said. "You know your body and if it's saying stop, then stop. Don't be so hard on yourself."

"Happy for you to walk with us though mate, if you want," Andy added, preparing to head off again.

"Nah, thanks, but I'll stick with this one." Olaf motioned

his head towards me. "We'll get there somehow, just need to work out how."

"Okay. Well, we're going to move along then," Sheila said. "Hope you're okay, Vicki, and hope to see you in Scarborough."

"Thanks, I'll be fine. No doubt we'll bump into you somewhere or you'll bump into us, one or the other. Enjoy the afternoon." They waved as they headed out.

"Enjoy walking the miles and creating some smiles," the attendant said as they closed the door.

Olaf looked at the guidebook once more.

"How about we walk to Hayburn Wyke then see how you're going." He grimaced on my behalf as I rubbed anti-inflammatory into my swollen knee.

"How far is that from here?"

"About six kilometres. Is that too far?"

"That'd be my limit. There's no way I can get to Scarborough. Check out my foot."

My right little toe had bled through the bandaging, which looked more dramatic than it turned out. With some dabbing and new plasters on, a quick foot rub, my feet were patched up enough to continue for a bit longer. Olaf's beautiful, big hands gave my shoulders a longed-for massage and I felt more uplifted than I'd felt all day.

"We can catch a cab or bus from there if you want. What do you reckon?"

"Yep. I think I'm good to go for a bit longer. Six ks is about it." I started to repack in readiness.

"Um, sorry folks, I couldn't help but overhear," the shop attendant said, "you won't be finding a taxi at Hayburn Wyke and no bus service either, love."

"Oh, no," I said. "What a bugger. But thanks for letting us know." I turned to Olaf pulling a 'what now' face. "Do we have a Plan B?"

"I'm going to need a few more minutes for that," he said.

He flicked through pages, sourced a bus timetable, consulted his phone, while I carefully put my socks and shoes back on. "It looks like there's a bus stop just over there. Perhaps that's our Plan B – get a bus from here to Scarborough. Does that sound okay?"

"Yeah, that's more than okay with me. It's getting better all the time."

"And it looks like the bus comes past here twice a day." He glanced at his watch, "And the next one is due in - three hours."

"What? Three hours? No way, that's too long to wait. So, is there a Plan C?"

"I'm going to need a *lot* more minutes to work that out but the way it's looking, you're not going to like Plan C."

Walking the whole way to Scarborough was increasingly looking like our only option; that was Plan C. And if that was to be the case, we'd need to get moving as our break had now blown out to well over an hour.

"Sorry to interrupt again, love," our helpful eavesdropper said, "I've been thinking about getting you two to Scarborough. Now, the buses run all day at Cloughton and there's one that'll get you to Scarborough. If you can just get yourself to Cloughton, that should see you right."

"How far is that from here?" I asked. "Please don't tell me it's too far. I don't think I could handle it."

"Let's see, about 1.5 kilometres on from Hayburn Wyke, you turn off the Cleveland Way and then it's about 1.5 kilometres inland. I think that'll serve you well," she added.

"So, how far from here to that turnoff?" Olaf asked.

"I'd say about seven kilometres from here."

"That's a lot better than continuing on to Scarborough," I added. "You've definitely saved the day. Thank you so much."

"No trouble, love. Glad to help," she said, pointing to something on a map.

What a blessing it had been stopping at the visitor centre, despite my initial Devonshire tea disappointment. Okay, it was more than disappointment, I was pissed off, but it had been completely overturned by our helpful local's invaluable knowledge. *Now happy, Jan!* was my new mindset, even though it was still an eight or nine kilometre walk to Cloughton, which was further than I'd have liked. As we strode down the path towards the Raven Hall Hotel, I knew I was going to feel every step of the way. But when I spied a way-marker displaying 17 kilometres to Scarborough, it was clear we were making the right decision and we'd still end up having a 20-kilometre day.

Along the cliff path, my body readjusted to moving again with the groaning rivalling any of those foghorns we'd seen earlier. Then as we'd started to settle into our rhythm, I noticed a sign for 'Tearooms' pointing off to the right; it must've been where Andy had hoped to enjoy a coffee. But as we neared, we could see it was deserted – not a teapot nor scone to be seen – and I'm sure Andy was pleased they'd stopped when they did.

We followed the narrow path through a field, past an old coastguard lookout and wartime radar station and, again, Olaf walked ahead. I cast my eyes up and could see the ruins of the 3,000-year-old royal fortress and one time prison, Scarborough Castle, way into the distance, confirming just how far away the town was. But I soon had to cast my eyes back down again as the clifftop path was strewn with uncollected hedge clippings, which created a slip hazard. Then there was a welcome change for my aching and swollen knee, bunged-up feet and entire body as the terrain flattened out for the next five kilometres.

The descent into Hayburn Wyke – our potential stopping point had we been on Plan A – was down more narrow and very steep steps. I clung to the slippery wooden handrail like my life depended on it and was relieved to reach the bottom in one piece. At the base, we crossed a footbridge and walked cautiously over leaf-covered stones underneath enormous chestnut trees.

The path snaked left, then right and suddenly became unclear which way to go.

"I can't face getting lost again," I shouted as Olaf disappeared around a bend.

He either didn't hear or chose to ignore me, so I hurried to catch up hoping he knew where he was going. He did.

Up and down we trekked, then a sharp climb brought us onto the clifftop flanked by open fields to our right and colourful cliffs to the left. It was a dramatic contrast to the dark and musty valley we'd just traversed and a welcome relief to be surefooted again.

"Surely that promised turnoff has got to be close," I said.

"Has to be," said Olaf, as he stopped to peer ahead. "That looks like a way-marker down there and a path heading off to the right. Gotta be it, surely."

"Better be." And it was. Cloughton was a mere 1.2 kilometres away.

The overgrown path headed inland beneath mature oak and ash trees and through fields dotted with large, round haybales. I wished I could've enjoyed it more but my feet were burning and my knee was resisting bending. I'd guesstimated it should take us around 20 minutes to get there but when we were still walking 40 minutes later, I questioned if the distance on the way-marker was a 'near enough is good enough' guide. Still, at least we weren't walking all the way to Scarborough and we'd have to be in Cloughton soon.

We emerged from a beautiful birch and ash woodland next to a busy main road and, this time, against Jack Reacher's advice, we turned right. There was a bus stop 50 metres along and, after waiting no more than two minutes, we'd boarded the number 15 bus, settled into our seats and were on the way to Scarborough. The scenery whizzed by as my weary body relaxed and I gave a silence thanks to our helpful local at the visitor centre. It didn't even bother me that the bus stopped at every single stop.

Toulson Court Bed and Breakfast was a kilometre walk from the bus station, which meant very stiff muscles needed to re-engage and my sore feet reactivate as we lumbered along that final stretch. Emma, our host, showed us our room and all the facilities with a delightful lack of military discipline. I removed my shoes immediately to inspect my aching and blistered feet to see the tapestry of plaster had rubbed off in parts and my right little toe had bled again.

As I ripped off the sticky remnants, my feet jiggled in glee at their freedom. My big toenails were becoming chalkier but somehow, had held together for the past eight days. I was sure they could hang in there for one more day. I didn't dare snip them in case they crumbled away but the other nails needed clipping as they'd been digging in to adjoining toes (plus more of their stained veneer would be gone). My blisters were in various states of healing and still needed careful dabbing, dressing and management. And then there was my ballooning joint which refused to deflate even with ice, anti-inflammatory cream and a good talking to. I could hardly complain to Olaf though; at least mine had cushioning inside. My bothersome right hip was worsening with barbs occasionally shooting down into my thigh. I'd get Olaf to massage it later.

Olaf had showered and washed items of clothing, which were now hanging in drying vantage spots all around the room, particularly on the heated towel rail. His beloved shirt hung by the open window, taking pride of place. I once again spent longer than I probably should've in the shower but I enjoyed its powerful flow and prayed for its restorative powers. Incredibly, tomorrow was the final day of our walk, although if my evolving idea worked out, our time on the Cleveland Way would live on.

We enjoyed delicious and abundant Turkish food at Az Restaurant, an unexpected and satisfying change-up to the food we'd had to date, and we headed back to our B&B while it was still early evening. It had been another very long day, even with the detour to Cloughton, so we were both looking for an early night and we'd heard thunderstorms were forecast tomorrow.

Day 9
SCARBOROUGH TO FILEY
15.5 kilometres

A peek out the window confirmed a bleak-looking day was in store and I wanted to pull the covers over my head and drift back to sleep as my whole body ached and my head was thumping. I was sure I'd had enough water yesterday – I didn't want another cramping episode – but the tension in my head suggested I'd underdone the hydration. Then I remembered it was our final day on the Cleveland Way and I was unsure how I felt. On the one hand, I relished the idea of getting to the finish line after the intensity of the last few months but on the other hand, I was saddened, almost anxious by its imminent absence. The tightly held goal to do the walk had been pivotal in my healing, so powerful in getting me through adversity and discover a strength I could never have imagined. And here we were, on the cusp of it ending. Maybe that explained the pounding in my skull – there were too many emotions clattering around in there.

Olaf must've sensed my agitation and gently stroked my back, then enveloped me in a comforting cuddle that said, *I'm proud of you, we made it, life is amazing.* I savoured the moment then started to cry but they were tears of relief and probably exhaustion. I'd pushed myself hard to get here and it was unsurprising to have a letdown; there was no controlling these feelings; they needed to come out and out they came for 15 minutes before they turned into tears of hope.

Eventually I collected myself and we headed downstairs for an early breakfast to try and beat the looming storms. We were first in the dining room again and eagerly loaded our bowls with the usual fruit, yoghurt and cereal. I had just taken my first mouthful when I heard loud singing emanating from the kitchen as Emma arrived to take our order for coffee and cooked offerings.

"Any requests?" she asked, pen and paper in hand.

"A long black would be great and scrambled eggs, thanks Emma," I said.

"Flat white, poached eggs and bacon, please," said Olaf, tucking into cereal.

"I meant any requests for Jim, my husband, singing in the kitchen," she said, smiling, "but I'll get cracking with your breakfast order lickety-split."

"Oh!" I was embarrassed. "I wondered who was singing in there." A small servery hatch slid open and Jim poked his head through.

"Morning!" he chirped. "Any requests?"

"Morning!" I replied. "No. Happy to hear whatever you want to sing." I was confident he was referring to song choice, not breakfast, this time.

"OK then. I've got a few songs in my repertoire. I'll see where the mood takes me." He slid the door down and launched straight into Frank Sinatra's *Somethin' Stupid*.

Emma brought our coffees and other guests drifted into the room. Some sang along with Jim's kitchen-bound concert and it created a jolly mood, almost like *A Day at the Proms* happening around us. Luckily, Jim sang well, otherwise it would've been awkward and unbearable as he selected tunes from his personal playlist.

Our delicious, cooked breakfasts arrived and we considered

our strategy for the day. We were totally underprepared for wet weather, so I opened our map to look for suitable shelter spots along the way. But all it showed was either exposed clifftops or open countryside, neither of which were ideal in a thunderstorm, while carrying metal walking poles.

"We could be in a bit of trouble," I said. "There's nowhere between here and Filey to shelter, that I can see."

"We might be okay," Olaf said, ever the optimist, "but we'll have to go soon. Filey isn't very far, so we might make it before the storm hits."

Our second coffees were delivered by Emma with an iPad tucked under her arm. She googled BBC Weather for an important update.

"Let me check when it's supposed to arrive," she said scrolling down her screen. "They're saying between 1:00 and 2:00, so you could just be lucky. But you'll need to crack a decent pace, mind."

"Thank you for that. I think we should get going soon," I said, "especially as we don't have any wet weather gear." Now a very foolish oversight.

"Oh. Right," she said. "Fingers crossed then."

"Yep, we definitely need to get a wriggle on," I reiterated. "So much for an English summer."

Emma chuckled, "Not just an English summer, a Yorkshire summer and all."

We headed upstairs, did a final pack with snacks and fruit and filled our water bottles for the last time on this walk. Back downstairs to quickly thank our hosts and be out the door and on our way, but Emma was waiting at the bottom of the stairs holding two waterproof ponchos.

"You might be needing these," she said. "They're not great but they're better than nothing."

"Oh, that's very generous of you," Olaf said. "We'll definitely be needing them. I can see it's already drizzling out there."

"And here's our business card," said Jim, emerging from the kitchen. "If you get caught or have any trouble at all, give us a call and we'll come and get you to Filey."

"That's a really lovely offer," I said. "I'm hoping we won't need to. But thank you."

With packs placed on our backs, we wrestled the ponchos on while still standing inside the entrance porch, then headed off on our final day through the streets of sprawling Scarborough. We tiptoed over slippery cobblestones, before descending to the beachfront with its vast expanse of recently raked sand, dormant amusement rides and copious fast-food outlets. But it was drizzling and dreary and the place was deserted. It was still early morning but I hoped, like Whitby, it would blast into summertime life later, full of screaming children, relieved parents and happy sideshow operators.

"So much for an English summer," I said again, smiling.

"Poor buggers," Olaf replied.

After walking along the lengthy seafront, the drizzle lifted and I couldn't wait to rip my poncho off. It hadn't offered much protection anyway and had only served to increase humidity levels underneath its canopy. My glasses were speckled with raindrops and almost completely fogged up; I was sweating profusely and we hadn't even left Scarborough yet. But once I'd escaped from the oppressive cloak, I quickly cooled down and appreciated the grandeur of the imposing and aptly named Grand Hotel sitting high on the headland overlooking the sea. We continued past the Victorian-era Spa Complex to the end of South Bay beyond the seawall, where a way-marker signalled 13 kilometres to go. I turned and gave the town one last look, then waved farewell to no-one, before exiting the beachfront via a narrow path up a steep, slippery climb.

Then the weather seemed to improve, the clouds dissipated and the threat of getting caught in a thunderstorm seemed to have lessened. But with Emma's words of warning still fresh, we picked up our pace and settled into a determined rhythm. Again, Olaf metaphorically pulling me along to make sure we kept to our self-imposed time limit. We scrambled under overgrown foliage arching overhead, before the gorse-lined path steered us back towards the subsiding cliff edge with signs on wooden railings reading, 'Sheer Cliffs. Take Care.' No need to worry, we would be taking care. Again, I turned for a final glance towards Scarborough, now gleaming in sunshine and I thought I saw the amusement rides chugging into action.

Around the Wheatcroft Cliff Golf Course, then through a wooded ravine, across inland fields and past houses with washing hung out, before a short walk along busy Filey Road. Initially, this pod of suburbia seemed out of place but then it struck me that we'd been able to blissfully suspend life's realities for the past nine days. It was something I loved about walking, when you were on the path, that was all you had to focus on and if you were walking again tomorrow, that then became your sole focus. No wonder it was 'Man's Best Medicine'; it was all about keeping things simple.

Along Filey Road we had to keep a close eye on the traffic, so when a dishevelled man appeared out of the thick, sloping woodland on our left, having climbed a rickety, wooden staircase, it took us by surprise.

"You gotta head down to Cayton Bay, you have to," he enthused in rapid-fire speech. "It's the best bay in Yorkshire, probably in England. You'd be mad if you didn't."

"Okay, thanks," Olaf said, as the man continued past.

When he was out of earshot I said, "I'm not so sure about that. Those stairs look treacherous and besides, I really want to get to Filey as soon as we can."

"Fair enough. But don't blame me for missing Yorkshire's finest bay."

A little further along and something wasn't quite right. Olaf referred to the guidebook and discovered we'd missed a turnoff and would have to backtrack. Having retraced our steps, we found the way-marker pointing down the precarious stairs where the man had appeared and we must've been momentarily distracted. At least we hadn't gone too far this time before realising something was wrong. I thought I heard Olaf mutter something under his breath about Osmotherley but I didn't quite catch it.

The small staircase needed careful negotiation, each footstep secured before the next was permitted, both hands gripping the wooden handrail until securely at the bottom. Then, our steep descent continued along the leaf-strewn, wide-stepped path, through the dark, cool heart of the woodland and then it started to rain heavily. We huddled under the thick tree canopy, which thankfully kept us dry, and shared a chocolate bar while deciding our next move. I wondered if this was the beginning of the storm and whether the crumpled poncho I shoved in my bag would offer any protection for the remaining 7.25 kilometres. Simply thinking about putting it on made my glasses steam up in anticipation.

"What do we do now?" I asked, not knowing what I wanted to hear.

"Let's wait a few minutes. It's already easing up, I think," Olaf said. "At the bottom of this path we should be able to see the sky and out to sea so we can decide what to do then."

We huddled for another 15 minutes until the rain suddenly stopped. I was relieved to have been granted a reprieve from wrestling with that dreaded poncho as, even without it, I was sweating profusely in this now-humid, post-rain environment. The dripping woodland was even more slippery underfoot and, as we recommenced walking, my deliberate strides made it very slow going. We headed for an opening in the thicket ahead and, once we'd reached the coppice opening, the sandy beach of Cayton Bay was revealed below. It was indeed a very fine bay, I had to agree with the man.

"Last chance to head down if you want to," said Olaf, pointing towards the beach.

"Haven't changed my mind," I replied, "still keen to get to Filey, without needing a poncho."

"Well, we might just be in luck. The weather comes from there, I think," he pointed to the north-east, "and it's looking a bit brighter. Fingers crossed for the next hour and a bit."

"They're tightly crossed. Don't worry."

The path led away to the right and I homed-in on a confirming way-marker as we continued along the undercliff out of the woods. Emerging from the cloistered and stifling forest was a relief, even though it had given invaluable protection and instantly, a gentle sea-breeze reset my thermostat. The now-expansive vista revealed Filey on the horizon and it seemed we might beat the thunderstorm and be enjoying a celebratory ale when, or if, it arrived.

As we'd found over the past nine days on the Cleveland Way, there was never much time for respite and once more, the path rose steeply along a fence up to the clifftop. The remains of two large concrete World War II gun turrets teetered precariously on the eroding edge and a third turret, which hadn't maintained its grip, was sprawled and broken on the beach below. I wondered how much longer these higher structures would remain perched up here and reflected on Olaf's musings about how things might look in 30 or 40-years' time. I'd be pretty sure the diminishing coastline would have them toppled onto the beach by then.

"Don't get too close to the edge, mind," a man said, appearing from thin air. "She's a bit soft underfoot at the minute."

"Okay," I replied, startled. "The erosion's really bad, isn't it?"

"No such thing," he said. "I've lived in these parts 40 years and there's no erosion. Got the photos to prove it. Them turrets were built badly and, well, you can see what's happened. But don't go saying it's 'cos of erosion – that's a load of codswallop."

"Oh, right," I said, unconvinced. "Well, I hope no-one's down on the beach should these topple over."

"Oh, they'll go at some stage," he added, then kept walking. He'd made his point and, seemingly in a hurry, was already several metres past.

"So, if it's not coastal erosion causing the cliffs to crumble, what is?" Olaf asked, but the man was out of earshot. "I'd love to have heard his answer; it would've been enlightening."

"We can only wonder," I said. But what I was actually wondering was how people kept sneaking up on us, then disappearing. What was it about Yorkshire?

We crossed more fields, then followed a road below Cayton Bay Holiday Village. It was school holidays and, despite the less than perfect weather, families were enjoying time together in the outdoors. Along the undulating clifftop, we passed several permanent caravans complete with white picket fences and feared for their precarious positioning, but I guess they *did* enjoy uninterrupted sea views – for now.

On through a gap in a hedge, then along the narrow path until eventually we left the caravans in our wake. An open landscape allowed our first full glimpse of Filey away to our right, and just when I thought it was smooth sailing to the end, there was another twist in the tale to this unpredictable walk. Instead of heading to Filey, the grassy path turned away from the village and it felt as though we were heading in the wrong direction. But we kept walking and two kilometres before we reached the township, there was a big surprise - an acorn-adorned way-marker was pointing back in the direction we'd just come, reading, *Helmsley, 175 kilometres.* So, was that the end of the walk and meant we'd now finished? Had we done it, was this it? But where was the banner reading, *Well done Vicki and Olaf* and the brass band and streamers awaiting our arrival? I didn't really expect that to happen but just stumbling on a sign wasn't what I'd anticipated either. I moved in for a short, sweet and sweaty celebratory kiss as Olaf snapped a selfie in one reflexive motion. A few hundred metres on, a large stone seat, exactly like the one in Helmsley at the beginning of the Cleveland Way, properly heralded the finish.

"We've done it," I said. "I thought we had further to walk."

"Me too," Olaf replied. "Still, we *have* done it. Feels amazing. But I think I've well and truly worn this out." He pointed to his knee.

"I can't believe how fit I feel now. Apart from my knee and my feet and hip, of course. I wish I'd felt this strong at the start of the walk, it would've been easier. Perhaps we should do it again," I joked.

"Not on your nelly."

"How about we walk to the end of the brigg and finish out there. I can't believe I'm saying that. My feet are screaming to stop but I'm not quite ready to finish."

"Okay. If that's what you want. We might as well, given we've dodged the bad weather by the looks."

We took some photos, even had some shots taken by a passing walker, then continued on to Filey Brigg – a long, narrow neck of land jutting several hundred metres out into the sea. It was a good decision to walk the extra steps to the edge; it somehow felt complete, standing there. Until only a few days ago, I hadn't given a thought to what might come next, what life would look like having completed the goal which had driven me for the last 10 months. But that 'Eureka' moment in Saltburn offered a new challenge and I was bubbling with excitement.

"I found this in my pocket in Osmotherley," I said, pulling the acorn from its safe space. "I have no idea how it got there but I figured it was a sign of growth. I made it my personal lucky charm, with me all the way. And with my hair growing at a rate of knots, I put it down to the power of the acorn."

"Would it matter if I said, I put it in there?" Olaf asked, hoping not to burst the apparent magic bubble.

"Did you? You sneaky devil. Why?"

"Because you embraced the whole acorn thing back on day one and I thought I'd tuck it in there for the duration. Couldn't do any harm."

"Well, I guess that means there was no divine intervention but it doesn't change the fact that I've had an idea and I'm going to set it free and see what happens." I threw the acorn over the edge and yelled, "I'm going to write a book."

"Oh, okay. I didn't expect that. Wow. That's great."

"It is. I'm really excited. It came to me the other night and I've been mulling it over ever since."

"So, a science-fiction murder mystery? No, it's going to be a bodice-ripping romance thing, isn't it?"

"You really are a goose." We laughed, then he grabbed me in a huge hug. I had his support once more. "I want to share my story. I think it'll help me process this journey we've been on and, you never know, it might help somebody else as well."

"That's brilliant. It'll be brilliant – whatever it is. I *was* thinking about what came next."

"Well, we'll have to get you a new knee first – that's the next thing in the short term. Then, look out!"

"Look out now!" Olaf yelled, as a huge gull swooped. "We need to get going if you're ready. Those clouds are rolling in and I'd hate us to get wet now."

"I'm ready. I'm really ready!" And I was. It felt good to have verbalised my idea and released it into the world and a big relief to know what was coming next. The giant void of 'getting on with life' now had a structure, one that didn't involve climbing library stairs or worrying about my ability to walk 175 kilometres. The next plan had emerged organically and felt just right. How I would make it happen was still unknown but in the words of Ralph Waldo Emerson, 'Once you make a decision, the Universe conspires to make it happen.'

With an underlying sense of urgency we slotted into our rhythm, side by side, hand in hand. I was awed by Olaf's capacity to nurture, support and encourage me, not just along this path but in life. Overwhelmed with gratitude at the joy of sharing my life with him, I started to tear-up. How on earth could I fully capture him in my book? The thought instantly halted the tears and instead made me smile – the Universe hadn't taken long to get the creative wheels in motion.

Across the Country Park we scurried, past St Oswald's Church, then stumbled on our B&B – Seafield Guest House. Our host, Jonathon, welcomed us warmly, showed us around and settled in for a lengthy chat which felt like hours but was probably closer to 15 minutes. I was desperate for a hot shower and excused myself as politely as possible while Olaf remained 'stuck'.

I took off my shoes and looked at the patchwork of tape and bandaging on my feet and marvelled that it had somehow worked. Obviously, there'd been the odd blister and sore spot, but my biggest concern, my toenails, had clung on and survived. As I unravelled the plaster binding my big toes, they popped up like meerkats in a 'ta-da' moment, proud that they'd done it, proud they'd survived the nine days of walking and I vowed never to take them for granted again.

The tiny bathroom proved a challenge but the shower's strong, hot jets more than made up for it. I lingered, letting the cleansing stream wash away the uncertainty of the last testing year. It felt wonderful, liberating, to have fulfilled this physical challenge but what was even more inspiring was to have found a new, emotionally cathartic one ahead.

Olaf finally extricated himself away from Jonathon and managed to manoeuvre into the miniscule shower space for his turn underneath the restorative cascade from the showerhead. I was sorting out our desperately-in-need-of-a-wash clothes when there was a gentle knock at the door. I assumed Jonathon must've forgotten to tell us something earlier and so took a deep breath as I opened it.

"It *is* you," said Sheila. "I asked Jonathon if an Australian couple had checked in and when he said yes, I knew it had to be you."

"Oh, wow! Yes, it's us. Good to see you," I said, grinning widely.

"What are you up to?"

"Well, Olaf's in the shower -"

"Not *right* now," she laughed. "Are you free for a drink or dinner later on, if you'd like?"

"We are. And we'd love to. Give us half an hour and we'll be ready."

"See you downstairs whenever. No rush."

"Will do. This is great. So glad we've caught up on our last night."

Emerging from the bathroom, I filled Olaf in on the plan and his smile was almost as wide as mine. He still found time to wash his beloved blue shirt even though we weren't walking tomorrow, got himself ready and we headed downstairs.

"Hello, you two," Olaf said, entering the reception room where Andy and Sheila were waiting. They stood up and we shared hugs.

"A perfect way to finish," said Sheila. "I'm glad we can celebrate together."

"It's meant to be," I said. "Now, I don't know about you, but I'm starving."

"I'll drink to that," Andy said. "Let's wander down to the seafront and see what's there. Jonathon has given a few suggestions but I'd prefer to see what we can find."

"Absolutely," Olaf said. "Lead on." And minutes later, we were enjoying beers and ciders in the early evening sunshine at the Belle Vue pub. We agreed the walk, whether over nine or 10 days, had offered a 'proper challenge', as Andy had described it.

"How does it compare to the Camino?" Sheila asked. "It's crazy, we live in Spain and haven't done it. It's seriously too busy for us. We like quieter walks, but ones that still push us."

"We haven't walked all of the Camino," Olaf said, "just the last 110 kilometres from Sarria to Santiago de Compostela. But yes, it was significantly busier than this one. Although we reckon this has been tougher; it's really tested us and it's been amazing."

And with that, I became teary and choked up. I tried to speak but words wouldn't come. All I could manage was to raise my glass and splutter, "To the beautiful Cleveland Way," prompting glasses to be clinked, and a chorus of "The Cleveland Way."

A couple at an adjacent table also raised their glasses and echoed our toast. They'd finished the route yesterday.

Dinner was at Bella Italia Ristorante Pizzeria, meaning pasta and red wine was plentiful. We chatted like we'd known each other for years and shared more stories of the unexpected challenges and joys we'd lived over the past nine, or 10, days.

"It's going to be strange not walking tomorrow," Sheila said.

"It's going to be sad," I added. "I know it's only been nine days but we've just hit our straps. It'll be weird waking up tomorrow and realising it's all over. Mind you, my feet are telling me they're glad to have rest."

"And my knee made it," Olaf said. "Now I'm happy to send it off in style. But hey, wait - Vick's had an epiphany. Well, she's got a new project lined up; she's going to write a book."

"Oh, that's great," said Sheila, "about your cancer experience?"

"Yes, about that but also about this walk and other things as well," I said.

"Brilliant. To your book and to the beautiful Cleveland Way," Andy said raising his glass.

"To your book and the beautiful Cleveland Way," we toasted in unison.

It was a short walk back to the B&B, where we said our good nights, knowing proper goodbyes would happen at breakfast. As I lay in bed, I felt lighter than I had in months and was asleep within minutes of my head hitting the pillow.

MORE TO SEE

I woke from the best sleep I'd had in ages with an eagerness and excitement for the next steps I was going to take – not along a walking path, but along life's path. The anxiety I'd felt in Helmsley, about my physicality and stamina, had been replaced by a new-found inner strength at having conquered, not only this walk, but a number of inhibiting emotions as well. And to add to the whirlpool, I felt an enormous sense of relief at being able to let go of the months-long striving, with almost obsessive determination, to make it to this moment and could now relax into a less intense way of life. I'd found a new, exciting purpose as we'd walked – my epiphany or 'Eureka' moment had appeared – which felt natural and now obvious and, despite being filled with apprehension about where to start, it gave me a different, creative focus ahead.

I realised then my whole cancer journey had, in fact, been a blessing. Of course, I wouldn't recommend it to anybody and would've preferred a different pathway but without the rollercoaster of the last 10 months I wouldn't have the courage to make changes and face the future completely out of my comfort zone. Life has changed, I have changed and, although cancer has taken a number of things from me, it has given me more in return. I now have a deep confidence and greater self-belief that

I can tackle anything and the sooner they're tackled, the better because life has no guarantees. So, no longer bound by medical appointments, physical restrictions or training targets, I'm free to pursue and enjoy a new cancer-free life and give myself unfettered permission to do so.

Olaf woke full of zest and we were both pleased not to have to rush to get bags downstairs, backpacks organised or rush for anything really. He put on his blue shirt and I wondered why he'd packed any other clothes at all. But I liked that the shirt was now inextricably linked with this significant trip with my repeated view of it from five paces behind.

Downstairs in the breakfast room, I busied myself with the usual buffet of fruit and yoghurt, while Olaf seemed distracted.

"Morning! Hope you slept well," Jonathon said, as he entered the room. "Coffee before or with your cooked meal?"

"Before please," I said. "Long black, thanks."

"Yep. Flat white for me, thanks," said Olaf, as a smirking Jonathon returned to the kitchen.

"Come on! I saw that wink. What's that about?" I asked.

"What wink? I don't know what you're talking about," Olaf answered.

"Come on! I saw it. What are you up to?"

Andy and Sheila arrived, interrupting my probing, looking relaxed and exuding an energetic aura. They'd slept well and also enjoyed the morning's slower pace without much structure. Jonathon brought our coffees then quickly returned with their newly placed orders.

"Okay," he said, commanding our attention, "it's a special breakfast this morning, thanks to Olaf here – I'm making cheese omelettes and I'll have them to you shortly." He disappeared once again into the kitchen as we exchanged glances amid a chorus of thankyous and Andy and Sheila continued their conversation.

"Please explain," I said to Olaf quietly, imploring him to spill the beans. "What's going on?"

"Right. Well, you know how I said I'd deal with our smelly cheese in Whitby?"

"Mmmmmmmmmmm."

"Well, I didn't end up throwing it out. I know it stunk but it was such a part of this walk, I thought it'd be fun to lug it along. Anyway, Laura wrapped it tightly and I've been hiding it since then. I was going to make some grand revelation or something when we got to the end, but then you had your acorn-throwing announcement and I totally forgot." I nodded, waiting for more. "Then when we got here, I remembered I still had it and when you went to shower, I asked Jonathon if he could get rid of it. He told me later, some of it was still okay and so we thought he could make cheese omelettes this morning."

"Well, that is definitely *not* what I expected. I can't believe you kept it hidden all that time, or that any of it is edible. That's amazing. What were you going to do with it at Filey Brigg?"

"I hadn't thought that bit through yet. I was hoping it'd just come to me and, in a way, it did, I guess, just a bit later on."

Jonathon juggled four plates, piled with toast and enormous, delicious-looking omelettes.

"Enjoy," he said setting them down on the table, "and thankyou Olaf, for supplying the cheese."

"A-ha," said Sheila, "that's where you come in. Thank you for the cheese. I'm not going to ask. Bon appetit!"

"Bon appetit!" we said.

It was the best omelette I'd ever had - the over-ripened cheese providing a certain piquancy I'm sure could never be replicated. We'd done justice to our cheesemonger's selection, who'd chosen perfectly and then we'd carried it with care. Olaf was right, it had been our companion and I loved that he'd woven it into the final moments of this walk. And then it hit me – these were the final minutes of this walk. In a silent reflective bubble, I thanked the Cleveland Way for being so diverse and beautiful, for the physical challenge through moorland and coast, for the intensely significant goal it provided through treatment and for revealing an enriching and exciting future. There was still more to do in life and so much more to see but at that moment I was fulfilled, content and definitely surprised at how well I'd come through it all.

EPILOGUE: OLAF'S KNEE REPLACEMENT

Olaf's knee replacement happened five weeks later and wasn't exactly smooth sailing, thanks to a reaction to the anaesthetic and the need for a second, smaller procedure. It set his recovery and rehabilitation back significantly and he was in varying degrees of pain for roughly 12 months. But he improved gradually and now, six years on, his knee is excellent and has a range of movement better than before. As for the pain, he says it's almost non-existent except occasionally when tackling a steep descending slope or a flight of stairs.

As for me, I'm healthy and well fronting up for an annual mammogram and touching base with my oncologist every year. The fear of recurrence is still present and, although I try not to worry about every twinge and ache, it's an ongoing battle. And in a quirky twist of events, I'm now a cheesemonger at the Smelly Cheese Shop in the Adelaide Central Market, selling every style of delicious cheese imaginable. I'm yet to master wrapping like the chap at Neal's Yard Dairy but am having fun sampling and learning about all things fromage.

Olaf and I are back enjoying our regular twice-weekly yoga practice and walking as much as we can, especially with Maya. We completed the Great Ocean Road Walk in April 2022, our first long-distance walk since the Cleveland Way in 2019 and, in late 2023, tramped New Zealand's Abel Tasman Walk and Queen Charlotte Track where a truly talented videographer (Cam Stables) beautifully captured our adventure and can be viewed at: www.youtube.com/watch?v=VNrcAof1py0. These walks always fill our souls with nature's nourishment and are a reminder of the joy of walking.

CHEESE TASTING NOTES

Innes Log
Unpasteurised goat's milk. Staffordshire UK.
Soft, dense and fudgy texture.
Bright, grassy, acidic, young hazelnut.

Coolea
Cow's milk; Cork Ireland.
Wax covered. Gouda-like texture.
Rich, sweet, caramelly.

Montgomery's Cheddar
Unpasteurised cow's milk. Somerset UK.
Semi-hard, crumbly and grainy texture.
Deep, rich, nutty, robust.

Appleby's Cheshire
Raw cow's milk. Shrewsbury, UK.
Hard, succulent yet crumbly texture.
Zesty, piquant, full-bodied, tangy, earthy. Clothbound.

ACKNOWLEDGEMENTS

A huge thank you to friends and family, especially my inspirational parents, for their enduring encouragement and solid support throughout. To everyone who has had some hand in making this book come to fruition, be it an encouraging word when it was needed, reading early drafts and offering feedback, or through the incredible online community brought together in difficult circumstances, thank you doesn't seem enough. I honestly could not have done it without them. My heartfelt gratitude goes to the providers of medical treatment and care, and those who continue to sustain my ongoing healing. And to those who've taken these journeys before and improved the paths for those of us who follow.

Finally, to Olaf who is my biggest supporter, inspiration and the love of my life. Without his unwavering belief in this book I would've thrown in the towel at the beginning of this journey and always wondered what if. But here I am. Having arrived at one destination I'm excited to look along the path to see what lies ahead.

About the Author

Award-winning, Adelaide-based writer Vicki Foote is a qualified art historian and Physical Education teacher who has worked in education, political media, television captioning, and magazine publishing. A relative latecomer to the joys of a long-distance walk, Vicki has now ambled up and down, across and around some great walks of the world including Spain's Camino de Santiago, Australia's Flinders Ranges, Cradle Mountain, and Great Ocean Road, the UK's Cleveland Way, and Abel Tasman Coastal Path and Queen Charlotte Track in New Zealand.

Having lived in London, Darwin and regional South Australia, Vicki is happy to call Adelaide, Australia, home where she lives with her partner, Olaf, and their Bernese Mountain Dog, Maya. She's always got at least one long-distance walk in the planning, with Western Australia's Cape-to-Cape Track, Scotland's Great Glen Way and the Sintra-Cascais Natural Park in Portugal high on her list.

She can be contacted through Foote Notes at www.footenotes.net.au

www.ingramcontent.com/pod-product-compliance
Ingram Content Group Australia Pty Ltd
76 Discovery Rd, Dandenong South VIC 3175, AU
AUHW022324051025
417590AU00012B/61